THE

EPISTLE OF PAUL

TO THE

PHILIPPIANS,

PRACTICALLY EXPLAINED,

BY

DR. AUGUSTUS NEANDER.

TRANSLATED FROM THE GERMAN

BY

MRS. H. C. CONANT.

WIPF & STOCK · Eugene, Oregon

Wipf and Stock Publishers
199 W 8th Ave, Suite 3
Eugene, OR 97401

The Epistle of Paul to the Philippians, Practically Explained
By Neander, Augustus
ISBN 13: 978-1-60608-682-7
Publication date 5/14/2009
Previously published by Sheldon & Co., 1859

INTRODUCTION.

In offering the following·work of Neander to the
American public, some brief explanation of its character
seems to be necessary. Many, who have only heard of
the author as one of the most profound scholars and
thinkers of the age, might otherwise be deterred from
reading it, by the supposition that it was merely a work
of learned criticism. Such, however, is far from being
the case. It was the beginning of a series of popular.
practical commentaries, intended to embrace the more
important portions of the Bible. Next to the Epistle of
James, which was completed, and a translation of which
we expect shortly to present to the public, were to follow
the Epistles of John, then the Gospels, the Psalms, &c.,
as rapidly as the public duties of the author would allow.
The surpassing excellence of the beginning makes us
deeply lament the loss to the church, through the recent
death of the great and good Neander, of so rich an addi-
tion to its means of understanding the Scriptures, and
one so happily adapted to the wants of common Christians. This, however, does not impair the value of the
separate parts, each division being complete in itself;

and we cannot but rejoice that, as he was not permitted fully to carry out his plan, he should have executed a part so appropriate as the closing labor of his life. Had he foreseen that these were to be his last words of coun- sel to his brethren in Christ, he could nowhere have found freer scope for all he wished to say for their in- struction, comforting, and edification, than in a commen- tary on the Epistle to the Philippians. One might al- most believe, such a fulness of pious feeling pours through its pages, that he had some such presage. Whether this were so or not, doubtless He to whom all events are known guided him in the selection ; and we may receive it as the dying legacy of one of the greatest Christian teachers with which God has ever blessed his church. May its instructions sink deep into the heart of the church, and bring forth fruit to the honor and glory of God !

In reading this commentary, one cannot but be forci- bly struck with the strong affinity between the character of Paul and that of his expounder. Different as were their outward circumstances and course of life, Neander seems to have had, in his own nature and spiritual sym- pathies, a perfect key to those of the Apostle. Hence it is that he has surpassed all others in giving the spirit of this Epistle. The grandeur of Paul's spiritual concep- tions, his personal aspirations, his inward conflicts, his magnanimity, tenderness, and humility, his all-absorbing love for Christ and for man, are delineated with a life and power which only a kindred soul in the writer could have inspired. His very manner bears the same stamp of resemblance. Impatient of the niceties of minute crit- icism, he breaks through the mere outward form, the shell of words and phrases, into the very heart of the Epistle; and develops its contents, not by a petty weigh- ing of particles, but by one broad, extended view of the whole scope of the Apostle's design and meaning. This he illustrates from Paul's history and character, his pres- ent circumstances and those of the infant churches; and the whole glows with the light and warmth of a deep personal experience of the Gospel. Thus, though the work is rich in the results of a learning as profound as it was various, the earnest and intelligent, but unlearned reader, can pursue his way unimpeded by any obtrusive lumber of scholarship. It is indeed a beautiful illustra- tion of what his friend and colleague, the evangelical Strauss, says of him in his funeral discourse: "He did not despise human knowledge; he sought for it with unwea ried diligence; he was a master in it; but he laid all the surprising treasures of his learning at the foot of the cross." To edify the members of Christ's body was with him a greater object, than to make a vain parade of his own superiority; as to be one with Christ was to himself, personally, an immeasurably greater object than all hu- man learning or honor.

One characteristic of the work, which adds greatly to its practical value, has also a special interest as showing

the author's character under a new aspect;—we mean
the comprehensive and accurate knowledge it exhibits of
men and their relations. It shows that he was no mere
recluse scholar, buried in the past, with no eyes nor ears
for the living world around him. It is indeed a prob-
lem, how a man who so seldom went beyond his study
and his lecture room, whose own relations to society were
so few, and his associations almost exclusively among the
learned, could have gained so much acquaintance with
human nature, and with the various forms and phases of
Christian experience. The solution is to be found in the
fact, that Neander had a heart as well as intellect; a
heart gifted by nature with the largest human sympa-
thies, and from early life penetrated by the spirit of Christian benevolence. Man his brother, man whom God had
created and for whom Christ had died, was to him an
object of unspeakable interest, and nothing was unim-
portant which affected his character and prospects.
Hence, from the little that he mingled with men he
learned much of man; and he applies the inspired instructions with a discrimination and point, which show
that no generic differences in human character had es-
caped him. It is a matter of no little interest, to know
what views of man were received from this study by a
mind like Neander's. It is plain that he cherished no
high-wrought notions of the natural goodness and per-
fectibility of the race. Yet he did not turn from the
weak and erring being with philosophic contempt, or

thank God that he was not as other men are. His was the earnest, penetrating scrutiny of a Christian philanthropist, seeking to know his brother's wants in order that Christian love might supply them. Though he was no believer in inherent human goodness, he was a firm believer in the efficacy of the great remedy for man's moral diseases. Hence the clearer perception of his ruined and lost state, only awoke more strongly the love which yearned to bring relief. The spirit of Neander's life and writings furnish sufficient proof, if proof were still wanting, that the clear recognition of man's entire moral perversion is the basis for all true love of humanity. His practical wisdom, as well as the tenderness of his heart, are beautifully exhibited in his treatment of the yet immature believer. The germ of divine life, planted in a human heart, is an object which engages all his interest. The causes which may obstruct its free development, as found in the various forms of self-deception, in the power of early prejudice, and not less in the over-hasty zeal or unchristian harshness of brethren, are touched with admirable skill. If his lessons of rigid self-scrutiny, trying as by fire every thought and motive of our own hearts, and of a fraternal charity, quick to discern and acknowledge and tenderly to cherish the faintest signs of grace in others, were carried into practice by every disciple of Christ, who can doubt the speedy increase of spiritual life, of unity, and of moral power in the church!

Another not less interesting point is the simply scriptural character of his theology, of the exhibition here given of the essential doctrines of the Gospel. Christ, the Crucified and the Risen, as the one foundation of the church, the living root from whom proceeds all spiritual life and growth; man as a sinful and lost being, depending for regeneration and sanctification on the influences of the Holy Spirit; the utter insufficiency of human works as the ground of salvation; a holy life as the necessary fruit of holy love; these, no man since Paul has more eloquently enforced than Neander. In developing Paul's theology, deep religious experience supplied to him that light, for the lack of which so many have misunderstood and perverted the meaning of the great Apostle. The natural man, and the spiritual man, designate with him radical distinctions of character. The tendencies of the natural man, however beautiful his social and even religious virtues to human view, are yet, as springing from self and ending in self, radically wrong; the tendencies of the spiritual man, as springing from God and ending in God, are radically right. But the spiritual man, and the perfect man, are not with him interchangeable terms. The Christian life is an unceasing conflict with inward depravity; that we persevere in this conflict to the end, the only reliable proof that we belong to Christ. The Christian's standard of character is perfection, is Christ; his ever increasing sense of unlikeness to this faultless model, the strongest evidence that he is becoming more and more assimilated to it. This sense of unlikeness, while it humbles and stimulates, does not disquiet the believer; for his confidence and his affections are placed on a nobler object than self, were it in a state of absolute perfection. The incarnate Word, the brightness of the Father's glory and the express image of his person, once humbled in humanity, now reigning in divine glory, is the centre of all his aspirations and hopes, the life of his life, his all in all. An affecting proof of Neander's personal consciousness of these truths, was given on the evening of his last year's birth-day. His pupils having, as is customary in German universities on such occasions, honored their beloved teacher with a torch-light procession and a eulogistic address, he replied by a pathetic confession of human weakness, and spoke of himself as a sinner needing forgiveness through the blood of Christ. The whole course of his inward and outward religious life corresponded fully to this expression. "As to be a Christian," says Strauss, "nothing but a Christian saved by grace, was all his desire in his inward experience, so in his calling he desired only to be a servant of Christ." The love of Christ to his people, as developed in the past history of the church, was his most interesting subject of contemplation. In his hands, Church History became not a mere record of the mistakes of the human spirit, but primarily, a record of the miracles of the love of Jesus. And often, says his friend, his voice trembled and his whole heart gushed forth,

1*

when narrating individual experiences of grace, exempli-
fying the love of Christ. What a beautiful illustration
of his own favorite maxim, " It is the heart that makes
the Theologian !" The modesty of his Theology is not
less marked than its scriptural character. Our knowledge of God and divine things, though all-sufficient for
our present need, in his view is necessarily fragmentary
and imperfect; " to be cast aside when we are raised to
the full vision of the life above, as the conceptions of
childhood are cast aside by the mature man." How
habitually this conviction was present to his mind, is
pleasingly illustrated by the circumstance, that when
called on for an autograph to accompany his engraved
portrait, he wrote for the purpose the words : " Now we
see through a glass darkly, but then face to face."

The closing scenes in the life of this eminent servant
of Christ, seem like the reflection of that conflict which
he so admirably depicts in the heart of Paul, between the
longing to depart and be with Christ, and the desire still
to live that he may labor for the salvation of his brethren. To labor for Christ was, as with Paul, his life on
earth. Apart from this work, life had no value, no sig-
nificance. While he lived he must labor; and even after
the hand of death had touched his long diseased body,
he still strove to compel its services in his appointed calling in God's kingdom. This calling was one which enlisted all the energies and affections of his soul. To be
the instructor of youth in the Holy Scriptures, and the

historian of the Church, was a high destiny; and his devotion to it had all the ardor of a ruling passion. His
history he had now brought down to the period of the
Reformation; and with a mind unimpaired by age or disease, and glowing with his theme, he was about entering
on the development of that central epoch of modern
Christianity, when the summons came to lay aside the
earthly for the heavenly. How his heart clung to his
life-work, is affectingly shown in the sketch of his last
hours by his attached friend and pupil Rauh. We give
the substance of the account.

He was at his desk in his lecture room, on Monday,
when the attack came upon him. Inured to pain, and
accustomed to master it by his powerful will, he per-
severed in completing the exercise; though the broken
tones of his voice, at times almost inaudible from de-
bility, forced upon his affectionate auditors the conviction expressed in the touching language of one of
their number: "This is the last lecture of our Neander!" He reached home in a state of great exhaustion.
But after some slight refreshment, he immediately resumed his usual afternoon employments. For three
successive hours, though often interrupted by increasing
weakness, he dictated on his Church History. Late in
the afternoon, the symptoms of dangerous illness becoming more and more marked, his anxious sister insisted
that he should give himself rest. But he could not be
persuaded to quit his work. "Nay, let me go on!" he

exclaimed: "can every day-laborer work as much as he will, and would you deny it to me!" At length he was obliged to yield, and allow himself to be conveyed to bed. The next morning he was forced, by the increased violence of his malady, to consent that his usual lecture should be deferred; "but," as he expressly added, "only for to-day!" From this time it was an incessant struggle for supremacy between the mind and the body. In the afternoon, he called imperatively for his reader;* and blamed his over-anxious friends for having sent him away, and thus interrupted his progress in a work with which he was engaged, Ritter's Palestine. He then listened to the reading of the newspaper by another pupil, with earnest attention; selected what he wished to hear, and commented on this and that of its contents, till at length a heavy slumber overpowered him. The next day also, the daily paper being read to him as usual, the mention of some occurrence in the Church drew from him an exclamation of humorous contempt at the modish spirit of the day; an expressive shrug indicated his dissatisfaction at another. This day he experienced a little relief, from the refreshment of a more quiet night, which encouraged his desponding friends. But on Friday evening the last ray of hope was extinguished. Paralysis, the result of his exhausting disease, seized upon the kidneys. The fatal hiccough set in, and allowed not a mo-

* An affection of the eyes, which had increased almost to blindness, had for some two years rendered such assistance necessary.

ment's sleep. This scene of distress continued four hours, without mitigation. Groans were forced from him by the extremity of his anguish ; and he was heard praying in a weak and plaintive tone, which drew tears from every eye, " Oh God ! that I might sleep !" But the energy of his spirit was not yet quenched. The next afternoon, though in an agony of pain, the longing to be again at work in his great calling seemed to awaken in full force. He insisted that he would no longer be confined in bed ; and with a feverish impatience, never seen in him before, ordered a servant to bring his clothes that he might rise. A pupil who was at hand vainly tried to soothe him. Even his sister's entreaties were of no avail, till she said to him : " Remember, dear Augustus, your own words to me, when I resisted the physician's orders, —' It is all from God, and we must yield cheerfully to his will !' " " True," he gently replied in an altered tone ; " it all comes from God, and we must thank him for it !" Through all the variations of his sickness, his wonted tender consideration for his friends did not forsake him. He would not allow his pupils to neglect their duties in order to attend upon him ; watched lest his sister should not take needful rest, and received every slight service with the most touching gratitude. Even when scarcely able to speak, from pain and weakness, he would make the utmost effort to express his thankfulness. One little characteristic trait deserves to be mentioned. His large income, always devoted more to others than himself, was

yet insufficient for his multiplied charities, so that he was
often perplexed and distressed when he found a new object of compassion which he had not the means of re-
lieving. He practised the most rigid economy in his own
personal expenses, that he might have more for others.
Every luxury was in his view a robbery of the poor. So
fixed were his habits in this respect, that when a little
champagne was offered him during this last sickness, he
promptly refused it with the expression, " O that is a
foolish indulgence !"

The final scene is one most characteristic of the man,
as well as one of the most striking ever witnessed in the
chamber of death. A wine bath had been prepared for
him, as a last resort. Refreshed and strengthened by it,
he was borne from the darkened room where he had lain
hitherto into his study, that cheerful little apartment
opening to the sun, which had been so long the work-
shop and the paradise of the man of thought. Here for
nearly twenty years he had studied and written. From
this spot had gone forth those great works which have
delighted and instructed Christendom. With thirsty
glances he drank in the full golden sunlight, of which he
was always so fond.* A spoonful of choice wine being
offered him, he did not reject it,—" a significant omen,"

---

* In this also, " a child of the light," as he sportively called himself
(ὀπαδὸς τοῦ ἡλίου) a few days before. " This I have,"—said he on that occasion,—*" in common with the emperor Julian ; but that," he added,
" Strauss must not know !"

says Rauh, "that the old order of things approached its
end." Ere long he murmured dreamily, as if at the close
of a long fatiguing walk with his sister, "I am weary;
let us now make ready to go home!" Just then the rich
sunset glow, pouring through the window, lighted up the
shelves from which looked down upon him the masters
of thought, with whom for so many years he had held
silent but high and endearing communion. Raising himself by a sudden effort from his pillow, he commenced a
regular lecture upon New Testament exegesis. Soon a
new image passed before his restless fancy. Imagining
himself at the weekly meeting of his beloved *Semina-
rium*, surrounded by his fondly attached theological pupils, he called for the reading of a dissertation, shortly
before assigned, on the material and formal principle of
the Reformation. He then dictated the titles of the different courses of lectures to be delivered by him during
the next session; among them, "The Gospel of John,
from its true historical point of view." His last thoughts
amid the struggles of death, were devoted to the great
labor of his life. Beginning at the very passage of his
Church History where sickness had arrested his progress,
he resumed the thread of thought, and in spite of inter-
ruptions, continued to dictate in regular periods for some
time. At the close of each sentence he paused, as if his
amanuensis were taking down his words, and asked,
"Are you ready?" Having closed a division of his subject, he inquired the time   Being told that it was half-

past nine, the patient sufferer repeated once more : " I am weary ; I will now go to sleep !" Having by the aid of friendly hands stretched himself in bed for his last slumber, he whispered in a tone of inexpressible tender ness, which sent a strange thrill through every heart : " Good night !" It was his last word. He immediately fell into a sleep, which continued four hours ; when his great spirit, in the quiet of a Sabbath morning, passed gently into the land of peace.—What a commentary on his own exhortation so lately uttered ; that " the Chris- tian should ever remember that here all is fragmentary, nothing reaches completion ; that even service in the cause of Christ on earth, is but the beginning of an ac- tivity destined for eternity ; that we must therefore not be so absorbed, even in labors consecrated to God, as to be unprepared to obey, at any moment, the summons to the higher life and service of Heaven !" He was so pre- pared, that when his ear caught the summons, he could drop the great labor of his life unfinished, lay himself down quietly upon his bed, and with a child-like " Good Night" to those whom he left behind, *slumber over* (as the German beautifully expresses it) into that higher life of heaven.

Before closing, the translator would beg of those con- versant with the author's manner in the original, as favor- able a judgment of her work as justice will allow. They can best appreciate the difficulty of the task. It has been her aim, not merely to give a faithful rendering of the author's ideas, in an easy English style, but to reproduce them, so far as possible, in their original form and mould. The elephantine march of his style suits, as no other could, to the great burden of his thoughts ; which, more-over, are so combined and *massed* together, that not only would the manner be lost by much breaking up of his sentences, but the connection and relation of the differ ent parts be seriously impaired.

H. C. C.

Rochester, N. Y.
Sept. 1851.

EPISTLE OF PAUL

TO

THE PHILIPPIANS.

If the Spirit of God has revealed to holy men of old the word of truth, that they might proclaim it for the salvation of mankind; if God has revealed himself through their lives, their discourses, their writings, as the depositaries of his Spirit; this is not to be regarded merely as an isolated fact belonging solely to the past. To us as living members of the body of Christ, as partakers in that fellowship of his Spirit, which unites the instant of the present with the whole progressive development since the first outpouring of the same Spirit by the glorified Son of man, to us, this should be no external, no foreign thing. The past must become to us the present. We need no further revelations. On the contrary, it must be to us as if the Lord had himself at this moment

spoken to us, inasmuch as he has given us the instruction required for all the higher necessities of
the present; as if he had himself said to us all
which it concerns us to know, in order to find con-
solation under present sufferings, the means of certain victory in all conflicts, the clue to guide us
out of all the perplexities of a distracted age safely
to our goal.   For the attainment of this object,
we must carefully investigate the precise historical conditions and relations under which these
depositaries of the Divine Spirit spoke and acted.
We must transfer ourselves into that past time, so
as to live, as it were, in the midst of the circumstances under which these holy men acted, and in
reference to which they spoke.   The objects of
divine wisdom in its guidance of the Church, we
perceive in this, viz., that divine truth has been
revealed to us, not in a law of the letter, not in a
digested summary of specific articles of faith, but
in this historical embodiment, in this application to
individual cases, to specific historical circumstances
and social relations, imparted through the instru-
mentality of individual men, who lived as depositaries of divine truth among their fellow-men;
who, in the common intercourse of human life,

testified of and revealed the divine, speaking and acting as men, each in his own peculiar human manner, though hallowed indeed by the Spirit of God. Thus was divine truth to be brought humanly near to us. Thus to our own spiritual activity, under the guiding and quickening influence of the Spirit of God, without whom nothing divine can be received or understood, was to be left the work of investigating the divine in its connection with the human; from the particular to deduce the universal; and again, by an application of this to the peculiar circumstances of the age and society in which we live, to reconvert it into the particular for ourselves; to detect in that which was said or done by the organs of Christ's Spirit, under the peculiar circumstances of the past, whatever is applicable for our use to the circumstances and relations of the present. Whilst, therefore, an humble dependence on that Divine Spirit, who alone leads into all truth, and unlocks the depths of his word, is an indispensable condition to the right understanding and application of the Divine Word in its human embodiment; so also is a careful attention to all the human relations. The word of God allows no slothful hearers; it demands all the powers of the mind and soul. Only thus can its treasures be brought to light. If we fail of discovering these treasures, and lament over the want of light to illumine the darkness of the present state, it is because we have not met the required conditions. We have none to reproach but ourselves. We may here apply those weighty words of our Lord, adapted no less to stimulate and encourage diligent inquiry, than for warning and rebuke: "He that hath, to him shall be given."

In an especial manner is this true of the Letters of the Apostles. In these we should find far more to instruct, edify, and guide us in all the relations of life, if we thus weighed the import of every word. May the Spirit of the Lord enlighten and guide us, that we may in this manner understand, and learn to apply, one of the noblest epistles of the Apostle Paul, written as no other could write, and presenting to our eyes the living image of the Apostle to the Gentiles!

First, then, we must bring before our view the peculiar circumstances and relations, under which Paul wrote this epistle. Zeal for the salvation of the heathen world had drawn upon him the extremest persecution of the enraged Jews, who

grudged to the Gentiles an equal participation and
equal privileges with themselves, in the kingdom
of God. To this was owing his apprehension at
Jerusalem, his long imprisonment in Cesarea Stra-
tonis, and finally, through his appeal to Cæsar, his
captivity at Rome. The issue of his fate was still
uncertain. In his imprisonment, he was far less
occupied with anxiety for his own life, than for the
welfare of the churches, scattered through various
regions, who through the dangers which beset their
Apostolic teacher might become unsettled in their
faith, deprived, as they were, of his personal guidance in this dark and troubled period. Through
his pupils and associates in the preaching of the
gospel, who now formed the living link between
him and these churches, and through his letters,
must the want be supplied. Among these churches
was that of Philippi in Macedonia. It was the first
church which Paul had founded in that country.
Its members had been witnesses of the ignominy
and suffering endured by Paul, on account of the
gospel, as recorded in the Acts of the Apostles.
They had witnessed the example he gave of bold-
ness in the faith, of devotion to the Lord, of triumphant enthusiasm in his service, his joyfulness in

suffering, and the wonderful deliverances wrought
for him by the Lord. This had served, in a special manner, to give greater depth and ardor to
their love for him, who was ready to sacrifice all
that he might bring them the glad tidings of salvation. They followed the example of their faithful teacher. As yet, indeed, Christianity had not
drawn upon itself the attention of the Roman civil
power ; nor had it become an object of persecution
through the state laws, as from its opposition to the
national religion must soon be the case, under a
civil constitution with which this was intimately in-
terwoven. Accordingly no general persecution had
arisen, and the churches in most regions enjoyed
peace. In this respect, however, Macedonia formed an exception. Here, from the very first, the
malignant hatred of the Jews, who were scattered
in great numbers through the commercial cities,
had been excited against the preachers of the gospel, and all who embraced it ; and they had not
wanted means for producing discord between the
believers and their fellow-citizens and associates
among the heathen. Although no civil laws as yet
existed against Christianity, still there were means
by which the heathen could, in many ways, dis-

quiet and injure its new converts, distinguished by
their life and conversation in so striking a manner
from themselves. In the history of modern mis-
sions the same thing is repeated, in the intercourse
between the new converts and their former heathen
associates. .The church at Philippi remained
steadfast under all these persecutions. Their faith
and love had been approved thereby. Neither
could they be unsettled in their faith, by the persecutions which had now befallen their Apostolic
teacher. They were conscious of that higher fellowship with him under all his conflicts and sufferings. His sufferings, and the dangers which hung
over him, but added new fuel to their love and sympathy. To manifest this to him they had sent one
of their own number, Epaphroditus, who might
also bring back to them more exact information of
his circumstances. We know that although the
right had been given to the Apostles, by the Lord,
to depend for their temporal necessities upon those
for whose spiritual welfare they labored, yet Paul
never availed himself of this privilege. As the
attracting and recovering grace of the Lord had
been exhibited towards him in so peculiar a manner; as it had transformed him from the bitterest

persecutor into the preacher of the gospel; he felt himself constrained to do more than others, called by Christ in the ordinary way, and gradually fitted for his service, and to forbear the exercise of a right to which he was equally entitled with them. Thrust, as it were, by force into the work, he would, by more abundant labor, endurance, privation, manifest his unconstrained love for his appointed calling.—(1 Cor. ix. 17–19.) It is to be accounted his gift, growing out of his peculiar nature sanctified by the Holy Spirit, that he was able to number himself among those whom Christ pronounces blessed, for having forborne marriage for the kingdom of God's sake. Not that he would call them blessed on account of the state of celibacy, in and for itself; as if Paul could claim any advantage over Peter, who in a marriage consecrated by the Lord, labored for the advancement of the same cause; but on account of the spirit which led them to abstain from marriage, that love which would offer up all to the kingdom of God. It was this which animated Paul, and impelled him to contemplate as a duty whatever might, under his special circumstances, serve for the advancement of his work, and to undertake it with joyful zeal.

It was for this also, that amidst the labors of preaching, he sustained himself with his own hands as a tent-maker. He experienced in himself the truth of the Lord's words, " It is more blessed to give than to receive." In order to avoid every appearance of self-seeking, and to take from the opposers among the Jews and Judaizing Christians every occasion of suspicion, he himself assumed the whole charge of his temporal support. Still the church at Philippi were moved, by their heartfelt love to him, to anticipate his wants; and knowing how difficult he must often find it to earn a main-tenance, they had several times sent sums of money for his necessities. ˙ Paul, though he sought no gift, yet, in view of the feeling which prompted it, could not reject the free-will-offering of love. This church had now once more manifested in this way their active sympathy for Paul, by sending to him Epaphroditus. This circumstance, and what he learned through their messenger of the condition of the Philippian church, occasioned the writing of this epistle. Its object was to express to the church at Philippi his gratitude and love; to re-lieve their anxiety respecting his own situation ; to give them a view of his Christian state and tem-

per in the midst of his conflicts and dangers; and
to bestow upon them the counsels and encourage-
ments suited to their peculiar circumstances.

We must now, therefore, direct our view to
Paul's situation in his imprisonment at Rome; to
his demeanor in his captivity, as the mirror of
the state of his soul, so far as we can learn it from
this letter; and to his counsels to the Philippian
church, in reference to their peculiar relations, as
furnishing suggestions applicable in numerous ways
to similar circumstances.

Looking first then at Paul's situation, we shall
perceive that this was adapted to produce great
variations of feeling. He had given his public
testimony for the Lord Jesus, and had made his
own defence. This defence had produced the general impression, that it was not as a disturber of
the public peace that this imprisonment had befallen him, nor for any other crime; but only as
the preacher of a religion hated by the Jews.*
Against this new faith, as we have already remarked, there existed as yet no state law. If now
Paul could triumphantly establish his innocence
in this respect, it would seem that his safety was

* Chap. i. 13

secured. But the Roman civil laws ever regarded
an individual as in some degree criminal, who
should seduce the citizens and subjects of the em-
pire to apostasy from the state religion; and
should attempt to make proselytes to a new faith,
which, if not condemned by an express law, was
yet in its nature opposed to the religion of the
state, and was not of the number recognized by
it as tolerated religions. Paul's case was, therefore,
by no means so simple a one. Many difficult ques-
tions were involved in it. At times, the impression made by his public defence would awaken in
him the expectation of a happy deliverance, and
that he might be permitted to visit the churches
founded early in his ministry, and among these
the church at Philippi. Again, the prospect of
death was before his mind. What then? Do we
find his soul divided between fear and hope, de-
spondency and joy, dependent upon the external
impression of these changeful circumstances, as is
wont to be the case with others in like situations?
No; one deep undertone of cheerful tranquillity,
of surrender to the will of the Lord, pervades the
whole epistle. We see the man, whose confidence
rests on an immovable foundation unaffected by

change of circumstances, a foundation which no
waves or storms can shake. He is certain that, in
one way or another, the Lord will conduct him
through these conflicts triumphantly to a glorious
end.* With joyful confidence, he approaches the
termination of a life singly consecrated to one
holy service. He is conscious of not having labored in vain, as a faithful preacher of the truth,
which he sees bringing forth fruit in the churches.
These, as for instance the church at Philippi, are
the living memorial of his devoted labors for the
Lord, as he himself expresses it in this epistle; the
witness that he has preached the word of the Lord
in purity; his glory before the Lord when, at the
day of judgment, that shall be by Him brought
to light which was here concealed; when much,
which here seemed to be somewhat, shall be exposed in its nothingness; and when much, that
was misjudged and condemned by the world, shall
be acknowledged by the Lord as his own. How
nobly does this spirit of Paul express itself in the
words of this epistle, where he exclaims:† "And
even if I be offered‡ upon the sacrifice and priestly
service of your faith, I joy and rejoice with you

* Chap. i. 19, 20.   † Chap. ii. 17, 18.   ‡ Literally, poured out.

all; in like manner should ye also joy and rejoice with me." We must endeavor to make clear the full import of these weighty words.—The Lord Christ is the one Mediator, between God and the sinful human race redeemed by him. Through him all, who believe on him and enter into fellowship with him, are taken out of the ungodly world and consecrated as a holy community to God. Thus do they all become one priestly generation. There is no longer the distinction of Priests and Laity. All are become, through him and in fellowship with him, what he himself is,— Priests before the God of Jesus Christ who is also their God, before his Father who is also their Father. Their whole life is a priestly calling; as Paul represents it, Rom. xii. 1, "a reasonable service," that is, a spiritual worship proceeding from the rational nature, the soul. Herein the whole spiritual life manifests itself as a God-devoted, to God presented self-sacrifice; every inward and outward act as done in fellowship with Christ, as performed in his name, pervaded by his Spirit, enstamped with his image, a thank-offering and a praise-offering of the redeemed, well pleasing in the sight of God. This being true of all the acts

of each Christian in his proper vocation, Paul regards as his own priestly calling the Apostolic
work; as his own acceptable offering to God, the
faith planted by him among the Gentiles and the
Christian life of the converted heathen world. It
is in this sense he speaks, in these words to his
Philippian brethren, of " the sacrifice and priestly
service of their faith" as his offering to God. It
was customary, moreover, to pour out wine upon
the altar, a so-called libation, as a seal of the offering. Paul, foreseeing that his own blood might be
poured out in his priestly office of proclaiming the
Gospel among the heathen, that he might be called
to testify to what he preached in the very face of
death, and to put the seal of martyrdom upon his
life's work, here speaks of the outpouring of his
own blood as a libation,—an offering of himself
upon the sacrifice. Thus, with joyful confidence,
the Apostle advances towards so glorious a consummation of his work. Far from needing solace
from others, he could call on the Philippians to
rejoice with him. Uncertain whether he was to
finish his captivity by the martyr's death, or
whether his life would be preserved to labor still
for the advancement of the kingdom of God upon

the earth, he was prepared for both, submissive·
in either case to the divine will. The will of the
Lord was his will. The result would show, in
what way it was the purpose of the Lord to make
his life most subservient to His own glory. He
was in a strait betwixt two,—longing to depart,
out of the conflicts of the earthly life, into the
peace of the spirit's heavenly home; from where
the Lord is seen only by the eye of faith, to where
in blissful nearness he becomes an object of sight.
Although Paul was certain even in this his earthly
life of union with the Lord, he was far from feeling himself satisfied with what he already enjoyed. Not merely from external conflicts had he
learned, that this is not the land of peace promised to the Christian, and sought for by his longing spirit. To those internal conflicts, yet more
severe, which the life of faith must ever sustain,
he was no stranger. Herein also had his Saviour
led the way; he who cried "My soul is exceeding
sorrowful even unto death!" and, "My God, my
God, why hast thou forsaken me!" One of his
sore trials he calls "a thorn in the flesh;" com-
paring it to the anguish inflicted by a thorn fixed
and rankling in the flesh. It was the painful ex-

2*

perience of his own human weakness, in contrast with the revelation of the divine glory, which at times was imparted to him. Thus was he taught to distinguish what is divine and what is human, what belongs to this life and what to the life beyond. Thus too was he to learn, that the land of heavenly peace, after which the renewed spirit sighs, is not to be found on earth. Although Paul, as his life and his epistles testify, had made great advances in personal sanctification, yet he was far from wishing to separate himself from the number of those, who as sinners seek in Christ for justification; far from holding himself to be a sinless saint. He knew well that he had still to maintain the conflict with sin, and that he must persevere in that conflict faithfully to the end, if he would stand before the Lord. We need only to hear his own professions, as when warning the Corinthians against a false security he writes (1 Cor. ix. 27): "But I keep under my body, and bring it into subjection; lest, having preached to others, I myself should be a cast-away." By these words he describes his unceasing conflict with himself, lest after having brought others to salvation by the preaching of the word, which through the indwelling divine power works independently of the preacher, and brings forth fruit to eternal life, he should himself be overcome by temptation and fall short of that goal to which he has conducted others. The figure, of which Paul here makes use, is taken from the boxing combats of the ancients. The body is represented as the antagonist with whom the boxer contends; implying a still continued resistance of the body, once the servant of sin, against the divine life in the spirit. Paul describes himself as one, who by unremitting effort makes his body, the organ of sanctification entrusted to him, serviceable to himself as the servant of Christ. This conflict with the body of sin, inasmuch as the whole outward life of man manifests itself in the body, designates in general the entire conflict still to be waged by the spiritual against the fleshly man, by the new man against the old;—and this in the case even of a Paul. Thus Paul, instructed by his rigorous self-examination, is far from supposing when he contemplates his own life, that he has already reached the limit of heavenly perfection, or that he could build his confidence thereon as if it were a life of perfected sanctification. "Not as if I had already

attained, or were already perfect," is his own
beautiful expression of his conviction, in a passage
of this epistle which we shall presently consider.
Paul, then, was conscious that the blessings pro-
nounced by the Lord: " Blessed are they who
hunger and thirst after righteousness, for they
shall be filled !" " Blessed are the pure in heart
for they shall see God !" were not as yet com-
pletely fulfilled in him, but were still, in a certain
sense, a promise looking into the future.   Moreover, although Paul had been elevated, in his perception of divine things, above others of his own
time and of all time; although he could claim
that single higher revelations, over and above that
which was to be the subject of general proclamation, had been vouchsafed to him; yet he well
knew that all this was but partial and fragmentary, far from that completeness of knowledge before whose light all which is called in this life
higher perception, prophecy, the gift of tongues,
shall vanish away. He reckons himself among
those, whose knowledge of divine things is like
objects obscurely reflected in a mirror, where much
still remains uncertain; a knowledge which, in relation to that of the eternal world, is as the

knowledge of the child, to that of the mature man. He was fully conscious, that when he should be raised to the full vision of the life above, that which he knew of divine things in this life must be cast aside by him, as the mature man casts aside the conceptions of childhood. The twilight of the earthly life of faith did not satisfy the aspirations of his soul, which thirsted after knowledge; and he longed to pass into that pure day of heavenly clearness, where our knowledge of God and divine things will be inward, immediate, a direct perception of that which is present, a knowing as we are known. We see then that, in all these respects, Paul was penetrated with the full consciousness that the hope which has reference to the future, not less than the present exercise of faith, constitutes the life of the Christian. Apart from this undoubting prospect into the future, the whole Christian life seems to him an effort without aim, a chase after a phantom, a deceptive show; as he expresses it 1 Cor. xv. 19, "If in this life only we have hope in Christ, we are of all men most miserable." For the life of others is directed towards some aim, higher or lower, of the sensual or spiritual life, which may

actually be attained on earth. But the life of
the Christian, with all its conflicts, labors, and
privations, has reference to an object which has
no reality, if it be not found in the eternal life of
the future. It is from this point of view that
Paul reproaches the proudly secure Corinthians
with having lost the consciousness of this distinction between the present and the hereafter, between the conflict of the earthly and the triumph
of the eternal life. In their spirit and conduct
they seemed as if already in possession of all
riches, enjoying full satisfaction, the contentment
of all necessities, with no farther warfare from
within or from without. With this he contrasts the
wholly different image of the Apostle's life (1 Cor.
4 : 8). "Ye are," says he, "already become full,
ye are already become rich, ye reign without us."
They were in spirit and conduct, as if the kingdom
of Christ had with them already reached its consummation; and they, as partakers therein, had attained to all riches, to the satisfaction of all their
desires. And would this were so, says he; would
they had already attained to this participation in
the perfected kingdom of Christ; for then, assu-
redly, the Apostles would not have been excluded

therefrom, nor would their circumstances be such as they now are. Thus he holds up before them his own life of conflict, in contrast with their false security, their unauthorized and groundless exultation. (1 Cor. iv. 9–13.)

Thus there was reason sufficient even for Paul, though rejoicing in conflicts for Christ's sake, and finding therein his glory, still to long after that perfect union with the Lord in the life to come. In earlier years, indeed, we find him constantly referring to the contrast between the earthly life of faith, and the consummation not to be enjoyed till the resurrection. But at a later period, especially from the date of his second epistle to the Corinthians, we remark in him an ever increasing consciousness, that, as a necessary result of the inseparable union of believers with their Lord, both in his sufferings and his exaltation, they also shall on their departure from the earthly existence enter at once on a higher life of vision, into a higher, more undisturbed fellowship with Him. Thus in the fifth chapter of the second epistle to the Corinthians, he in this view represents the abiding in the flesh as an absence from the Lord, that is, from the immediate vision of Christ; while the state which follows, entered through death, through the laying off of the earthly life, is a being at home with the Lord——(2 Cor. v. 8). He expresses the same conviction in this epistle to the Philippians. Christ is his life.* He distinguishes life in this sense from his life in the flesh.† Christ is his true life; he has no life except in him, none apart from him. In him that which alone he calls life, has its being; it has its root in union with Him. And as Christ, having laid aside human infirmity, having risen and ascended to Heaven, now reigns triumphant in the Divine Life, living in the power of God a life exalted above the reach of death; so also is this true of the life of the believer, as being one with His own, yea one with Himself. And hence Paul concludes, that although even now, while abiding in the flesh, he has Christ for his true life; yet death is for him gain, inasmuch as through the laying off of the earthly existence, this true life, which has its being in Christ, shall be freed from the checks, hindrances, and disturbances by which it is still clogged, and shall attain to its complete development. He knows, that with his departure from the earthly life, will commence his "Being

* Chap. i. 21.   † Ver. 22.

with Christ"* in that more perfect sense, his presence with Him as an object of immediate vision. Hence this is the goal of his desires.

But there are two mistakes, against which the example of the Apostle warns us, viz. : the declension, on the one hand, of that longing after the blessedness to come, which, as we have seen, is inseparable from the very nature and essence of the Christian life ; and on the other, such a one-sided morbid predominance of this desire, as to weaken the exercise of patient submission to the will of the Lord. As to the first, we remark, that it is not alone in the enjoyment of earthly gratifications, which we should ever remember are in their nature transitory and but a shadow and pledge of those higher, eternal, heavenly joys, that the Christian may suffer the loss of this heavenward desire. Even his activity, in a calling entrusted to him for the promotion of the kingdom of God, may likewise so absorb him as to obscure the consciousness that he has here no abiding home, that his native country is in Heaven. He labors as if this work upon earth, which is but the beginning of a higher activity destined for eternity, were to be consum-

* Chap. i. 23.

mated here, as if it were already the work of eternity. Hence the thought that here all remains
fragmentary, that nothing reaches completion,
nothing attains to its end, withdraws itself from
him; and death surprises him in the midst of his
labors, consecrated though they be to God, as an
unexpected unwelcome guest, who finds him unprepared. He is called away before he has finished
his account; and instead of following joyfully the
summons to a release from the sufferings of time,
his heart clings fast to that earthly scene of labor
which he too reluctantly quits, to those happy results of his labors on which he has set too high a
value. Here may be applied the admonition of
the Lord: " Rejoice not that the spirits are subject
unto you, but rather rejoice that your names are
written in Heaven." This heavenward longing is
ever the salt of the Christian life, amidst all sor-
rows, all joys; in every season of repose, in every
labor. But on the other hand, this very desire, in
itself perfectly right, but needing to be restrained
by submission to the holy will of God, and by
fidelity to the calling appointed us in this earthly
life, becomes itself an error when it oversteps these
boundaries. Thus arises a one-sided direction of

feeling, an impatient haste for the call, which should be waited for with a steadfast unfaltering patience. In this undue, all-engrossing longing after the eternal, the importance of the earthly life and of its duties, connected as they are with the eternal, is forgotten. Earthly joy, and earthly labor, lose the proper value assigned them in the divine arrangement. That which the goodness of God has given us for the moment, as an earnest and a preparation for the higher joys of the future, is impatiently and unthankfully contemned. The consciousness is wanting, which should be ever present with the Christian, that for the redeemed united in fellowship with Christ, even here below, the earthly of whatever name, whether it consist in receiving or in doing, whether it be enjoyment or labor, is transformed into the heavenly. The temper of mind, which Paul's words exhibit, holds the just medium between these two extremes. The longing after the life of eternity, after the immediate society of the Lord, continues to be the ground-tone of his soul, which no other can overpower. Through all the pressure of his labors in the service of God, this longing after the heavenly rest is not smothered, is not crowded from his

heart. But he is far from an over-hasty impatience,
which cannot await the end of the earthly conflict;
far also from that more refined selfishness, which
cannot endure to strive and labor longer for the
salvation of others, and be still deprived of the
quiet enjoyment of heavenly blessedness. Though
to depart from the earthly life, and to be present
with the Lord in a perfect personal union, be the
goal of his desires; he is yet ready to deny this
desire, the offspring of what is noblest in man, in
order to labor still upon the earth and to strive
for the salvation of his brethren. If it may serve
for the advancement of the work entrusted to him
by the Lord, he is willing yet longer to forego the
object of his wishes, and to be still a wanderer
upon the earth. Love to his brethren, who may
need him for their salvation, enables him to present
this offering willingly; and thus drawn hither and
thither by these two directions of his desires, he remains submissive in either event to the will of the
Lord. But one desire remains fixed and unwaver-
ing, to which all others must yield, viz.:—That
Christ may be glorified through him, be it by life
or by death. Let us hear his own noble words:—
" As I earnestly expect and hope, that in nothing

I shall be put to shame; but that with all bold-
ness, as at all other times so also now, Christ may
be glorified in my body, whether it be by life or
by death. For Christ is my life, and death is gain.
But if my life in the flesh is fruitful for my work,
—then I know not which to choose. For I am in
a strait betwixt the two; desiring to depart and
to be with Christ, for this is far better."* Still he
gives that the preference, which may most subserve the welfare of the churches which he has
founded; and hence he adds: "But to abide in the
flesh is more needful for your sake." His love to
the churches inspires him, at this moment, with the
confident expectation (which indeed as he well knew
might prove illusive, but which as we have reason
to believe, was fulfilled by his release from his first
imprisonment at Rome) that God would again restore him to their society, for the strengthening of
their faith and the furtherance of their joy. "And
having this confidence, I know that I shall remain,
and shall continue with you all, for your furtherance and joy in the faith; that your glorying on
my account may abound in Christ Jesus (i. e. the
exulting joy which Christ should bestow upon

* Chap. i. 20–23.

them by the restoration of Paul to their society)—
through my coming again to you."

We here observe in Paul the example of submission to the divine will, both in doing and in
suffering, in self-sacrifice and self-preservation.
Surrendering his own will, he is ready for whatever God may appoint, be it life or death, as may
best promote the work committed to him. Filled
with longing after the home of heaven, he yet
seeks not death. For the good of the churches he
willingly remains on earth. Only in the faithful
performance of the duties of his calling is death to
him a divine gift, to be joyfully received from the
hand of his Heavenly Father. Thus, in life and
in death, it is alike the same operation of self-denying love. This example of Paul has primary
and immediate reference to the martyr's death, the
genuine Christian martyrdom purified from all ad-
mixture of fanaticism. But is it not also applicable to death under all circumstances, and in the
ordinary course of nature? In that case too, there
may be either that spirit of selfish impatience,
which, though it ventures not presumptuously to
sever the thread of the earthly life, is not willing
to endure it longer; or that selfish love to the

PHILIPPIANS. 47

earthly life, which clings to this with its whole strength, which cannot let it go when the call of God requires. Thus, in both these respects, does Paul's example of a love consecrated to God in self-sacrifice and self-preservation, find an application here. Thus should each Christian become, in respect to living and dying, one with him in spirit, though his calling may not lead to the martyr's death.

Furthermore, we here observe in Paul that higher degree of self-renunciation, which manifests itself not in the relinquishment of temporal earthly interests, which could have no attraction for a Paul, but in the relinquishment of the higher interests of the immortal spirit. It is a heavenly aspiration, which enkindles the lofty soul of the Apostle. His desires reach beyond the narrow limits and perplexities of the earthly existence after the immediate vision of Christ, in him to find the full satisfaction of all the wants of the higher life. This to his spirit would be the highest good. Yet even this he foregoes. He is ready to relinquish what is dearest to himself, to forego the satisfaction of that heaven-born desire, to abide still longer in the strange country, to labor still upon

earth, striving and suffering for the welfare of
others. What is best for the churches, for the
furtherance of God's kingdom upon the earth, is
more to him than what is best for himself. Now
this example is not to be restricted to its merely
literal application to a precisely similar case, viz.:
when one who is penetrated with longing for the
heavenly father-land, is yet obliged to bear the
load of the earthly life for the welfare of others.
It may in its spirit be applied to every case, where
the Christian is called on to relinquish a course of
life most favorable to his own spiritual interests, a
life of tranquil and collected thought consecrated
to devotion; and to plunge into a whirl of business, toil, and conflict alien to the higher inclinations of his soul, but where he is appointed to labor because the salvation of others requires it.
In this respect also, Paul furnishes for our imita-
tion an example of self-denying love, which shuns
no sacrifice for the good of others. How often
have Christians, who should be the salt of the
earth, by withdrawing themselves from its corrup-
tion acted in contrariety to this example!

Let us present still another view in which all
Christians have an interest. While Paul stands

thus between .ife and death, whereon is his confidence grounded? He, if any one, was a faithful
laborer in the work of the Lord. He was conscious of having labored more than all others in
the proclamation of the gospel. But he knew at
the same time that this was not his own work, but
the grace of God accomplishing all through him;
as he himself says: "I have labored more abun-
dantly than they all; yet not I, but the grace of
God which was with me." When higher considerations demanded his self-justification, against sus-
picions which might shake the confidence of the
churches in him, he could indeed recount what he
had done and suffered above others for the cause
of the Lord (2 Cor. xi. 22, 23). He could appeal
to the memorials of what he had endured in the
cause of Christ, in whose fellowship he suffered,
and whom he followed in his sufferings; to the
marks enstamped in his body by the Lord himself
(such as soldiers and servants were accustomed to
bear) as proofs that he was Christ's servant. (Gal.
vi. 7). Still, when looking towards the close of
his earthly course, he reviewed his life so abundant
in labors and sufferings for the Lord, as it now
spread out before him, he felt that he could not

rest his confidence on what he had himself done.
All seemed marked with imperfection. He was
constrained to forget what he had already accomplished, and to fix his eye upon what still remained
for him to do. It was with him a law, to forget
what was already done, what lay behind, and to
press continually forward towards the prize of the
heavenly calling. It may, at first view, seem
strange, that Paul expresses himself so doubtfully
on the great point, whether he shall attain to the
victor's crown of life, shall share in the blessedness
of the resurrection. It seems to be in conflict with
that divine confidence which breathes through the
whole epistle, and which he expresses elsewhere in
regard to the object of his hope; as e. g. in 2 Tim.
iv. 8: " I have fought a good fight, I have finished
the course, I have kept the faith." But this conflict belongs to the nature of the Christian life, and
is ever recurring in the experience of the believer.
Does the Christian look away from himself to his
Redeemer, to the delivering grace assured to him,
the unchangeable word of promise; the goal towards which all his efforts tend, seems then an object of perfect certainty. Does he, on the other
hand, test his own life by the standard of perfect

holiness; his confidence then finds no firm ground.
Defects and blemishes present themselves everywhere to his view; and this all the more the
farther he has advanced in holiness, the more his
sight has been sharpened by the power of the Holy
Spirit, to recognize the model of divine holiness in
its application to himself, to test by comparison
with this pattern his inner and outer life in its
nakedness and poverty, to penetrate into the hidden windings of his own heart. Hence Paul expresses himself so doubtfully in reference to what
he is in himself, and has himself accomplished.
What he has performed seems to him nothing, and
he only looks forward to that which remains to be
done. He is penetrated with the consciousness,
that he is yet far from having attained perfection.
But the ground of his confidence is this—that
Christ has taken him into fellowship with himself,
that Christ has apprehended him; and hence he
hopes, that as he has been apprehended of Christ,
he also shall apprehend the prize set before him
by Christ. He knows that Christ, by whom he
has been apprehended, will not leave unfinished
the work he has himself begun in him; but, if he
truly surrenders himself to his hands, will conduct

it through all conflicts to a glorious completion.
Let us hear his own brief, expressive words: "Not
as though I had already attained, or were already
perfect; but I follow after, if I may apprehend
that for which I am apprehended of Christ Jesus."
So important does Paul deem it to set forth, in the
clearest light, this truth drawn from his own self-
consciousness and from his Christian experience,
and to bring it home to the Christian as a warning
against self-satisfaction, self-righteousness, and spiritual pride!   Hence he adds yet again: "My
brethren, I count not myself to have apprehended.
But this one thing I do; forgetting the things
which are behind, and reaching forth unto the
things which are before, I press towards the mark
for the prize of the high calling of God in Christ
Jesus."   Paul was conscious in himself of the utter
insufficiency of man's own righteousness, not merely of that to which the vital principle is yet wanting, that which precedes regeneration and exists independently of Christianity; but of that also which
possesses already in faith the true element of sanctification, without having as yet brought this to
complete development and realization.   Hence, the
only immovable ground of his confidence is Christ,

by whom he has been apprehended; and whom
he, surrendering himself wholly to his hands, seeks
ever more to apprehend and to appropriate as his
own. Looking away from himself to Christ, his
assurance is complete; looking back upon himself,
he must doubt and waver; and thus he is driven
to look away from himself, and to cling more and
more firmly to Christ, from whose love nothing can
separate him. It is the righteousness of God in
Christ which alone avails for him, and is all-sufficient for him; as expressed in the words of this
epistle, "The righteousness which is of God by
faith." To him Christ is all. All centres in this
one point, that we enter into his fellowship and
make it more and more our own; that we follow
him by bearing the cross, thus following him as
crucified for us; that in fellowship with him we
die to sin, to self, and to the world; following him
in the entire renunciation of selfish and earthly interests, not shunning to partake in the fellowship
of his sufferings; and following him also as the
Risen One, experiencing in ourselves the power
of his resurrection—the resurrection to an imperishable and divine life above sin, death, and nature, proceeding from him to us, inasmuch as he

has apprehended us and we apprehend him. So
Paul expresses it, in a passage which we must more
particularly consider hereafter: "That I may know
him and the power of his resurrection and the
fellowship of his sufferings, being made conforma-
ble unto his death; if by any means I might attain
unto the resurrection of the dead." We have already explained how the Apostle could here express himself with so much apparent doubtfulness,
consistently with his divine assurance of faith.

It was the greatest joy of the Apostle, that his
imprisonment must necessarily serve for the furtherance of the Gospel; since it was becoming
more and more known, that no guilt of any kind
could be imputed to him, that it was but his zeal
for the faith which he preached that had drawn
upon him all his sufferings. A cause, to which a
man like Paul felt constrained to offer up everything, could not fail to command attention. To
this was added the impression necessarily made
upon those, who were witnesses of the enthusiasm
with which he testified in behalf of the Gospel, of
his steadfastness, and of his whole course of life.
The knowledge of this had spread, as he intimates,
by means of the soldiers from the imperial guard

(the *castris praetorianis*) who held watch by turn
in his dwelling, among their comrades and from
these still more widely. Other Christians were
stimulated by Paul's example to preach the Gospel with similar zeal, and to bear their testimony
with like fearlessness. Thus increased the proclamation of the truth.

But Paul himself makes a great distinction
among these preachers of the Gospel. Thus, when
expressing his joy at the increasing promulgation
of the Gospel, he says, "Some indeed preach Christ
from envy and strife; but others also from good-
will: the one out of love, knowing that I am set
for the defence of the Gospel." The latter, he
means to say, connect with their love to the Gospel also love to himself. They know that they
can cause him no greater joy, than by laboring
that the Gospel may be promoted by his imprisonment; for they well know that this is the one object of his life, and that he himself regards it as
the divinely appointed end of all that he is to do
and to suffer in life. "But the others," he proceeds to say, "out of party spirit, not sincerely,
supposing to add affliction to my bonds." The
first is clear. But who are those who sought, by

the preaching of the Gospel, to add affliction to
Paul's imprisonment, and whom he charges with.
insincerity?   We must here take into view what
he afterwards says in reference to this distinction,
viz. that by the one class Christ was preached in
truth, by the other only in appearance.   Are we
to suppose that these men, without personal love
to the Gospel, without personal conviction of its
truth, preached Christ for no other reason than to
add to the hardship of Paul's situation, and to
bring him into greater danger by the wider exten-
sion of the Gospel in Rome ; thus rendering him,
as the origin of it all, more obnoxious to the Roman civil power?   It appears at once how unnat-
ural, and intrinsically improbable, is such a supposition.   If they could thus bring Paul into greater
peril, they would by so doing plunge themselves
into equal danger.   Can it be imagined that one
would play so hazardous a game, simply from hatred to another?   He who at that time did not
himself believe in the Gospel, must be enlisted
against it; and would certainly not have given
himself up to the business of preaching it, merely
as the means to another end. We must seek, then,
another explanation of this difficulty.   When it is

said of an individual that he preaches the Gospel
only in appearance, this need not be understood
as necessarily meaning that he has no concern
whatever in regard to the subject of his preaching;
that he has no personal interest in it, no conviction of its truth, that he makes use of it only as a
means to another end.   It may mean that he
preaches it, not in its purity and completeness, but
mingled with foreign elements; that although an
interest in it cannot be denied him, yet this is not
perfect and unalloyed.   In this sense it might be
said of such an one, that he does not preach the
Gospel sincerely.   Paul might therefore express
himself thus, in regard to persons who testified of
the Gospel of Christ from real conviction; yet
did not preach the whole, unmixed, pure Gospel
in its completeness, but an adulterated, mutilated
Gospel.   And when, moreover, he says of such
that they were actuated by party zeal and hatred
against him, desiring to add new affliction to his
sufferings; it is not necessary to understand by
this, that their witness for the Gospel was mere
pretence, a form of hypocrisy to which the circumstances of the time afforded no occasion and
no ground; but that their ruling motive in

preaching was not pure love to the Lord, that it
was their aim, consciously or unconsciously to
themselves, by their manner of preaching to give
offence to Paul, and to raise up for themselves a
party against him.

If now we look farther into the history of the
development of Christianity in this its earliest period, and investigate more minutely, in the history
of the Apostolic church, the peculiar relations and
opposing influences under which Paul's labors
were prosecuted, we shall soon be in a position to
determine with greater exactness what we have
here remarked in general. We know that Paul
had to contend with opposers, to whom all that
has here been said is applicable. There were
those who did indeed acknowledge and preach
Jesus as the Messiah, but a Messiah in the Jewish
sense; who acknowledged him, not as that which
he has revealed himself to be, the only ground of
salvation for man; who in connection with the one
article of faith, that Jesus was the Messiah promised in the Old Testament, still adhered to the
Jewish legal position; who understood nothing
of the new creation of which Christ was the au-
.thor, and to whom faith in Jesus as the Messiah

was only a new patch upon the old garment of
Judaism. These were the opposers, with whom
we so often find Paul contending in his Epistles.
Of such he might justly say, that they preached
the Gospel not purely and sincerely, but only in
appearance; for they were indeed far more concerned for Judaism than for Christianity, and their
converts became rather Jews than Christians. Of
such he might also say, that they sought to form a
party against him, and to add affliction to his
bonds; for these persons everywhere seem chiefly
animated by jealousy of Paul, through whom the
Gospel was preached to the heathen world as freed
from all dependence upon Judaism, and standing
upon its own foundation. They oppose themselves to him on all occasions, contest his Apostolic dignity, seek to encroach on his sphere of
labor, to draw over the people from him to themselves, from that pure and complete Gospel to
their own mutilated one. And it need not sur-
prise us to meet such even in Rome; for Paul's
Epistle to the church at Rome, written some years
previous to his imprisonment there, shows us in
this church, consisting chiefly of Gentile converts,
a small party of such judaizing Christians who

were in conflict with the rest. It was a matter of
course, then, that when the pure 'Gospel in the
sense of Paul was preached by the one party,
the other, provoked to rivalry, should rise up in
opposition and seek to give currency to their own
corrupted form of the Gospel.

We must now endeavor to understand fully
Paul's position towards these opposers. Rightly
understood, it will furnish an important rule for
our own application in many cases. In the first
place, it is clear that these men were personal
enemies of Paul; and that in their efforts to promote the Gospel, their object was to frustrate the
labors of the Apostle, and to form a party of
their own in opposition to him. What self-renunciation must it then have required, to enable Paul
to rise so entirely above this personal relation,
that forgetting the design against himself he can
rejoice with his whole heart that the One Christ,
whom it is his sole desire to glorify, is preached,
even though it be by his personal enemies! Thus
everything pertaining to self gives place to that
all-absorbing love to the Lord, and to those for
whom He gave his life. How rare are the exam-
ples of a love so heaven-like, so purified from all

selfishness! One may even be animated by real
zeal for the cause of the Lord, and yet that zeal
be impaired by personal considerations. If others,
who from unfriendly designs against him personally labor to frustrate his efforts, are used as instruments for the promotion of the same holy
cause,—he cannot rejoice over it. That this is accomplished not through himself, but through
those who are acting against him, weighs more
with him than the common interest of Christ's
cause; and instead of giving him joy, it becomes
a source of vexation, jealousy, and envy. He is not
concerned alone that Christ should be preached,
but that He should be preached through him; or
at least through his followers, through those who
in every respect harmonize with him, and acknowledge him as their teacher in Christianity.
Least of all can he endure it, when Christ is
preached by those who take a hostile attitude
towards himself; whose most zealous effort it is to
lessen his reputation, to throw suspicion on him as
a teacher, to draw men away from him. To this
course of conduct, which we so frequently observe
among men, the Apostle's self-denying zeal forms
the most striking contrast. He acted in accord-

ance with the principle which he himself lays down in 1 Cor. iii. 21, showing in what light the preachers of the Gospel should be regarded. "Let no man," says he, "glory in men;" the highest, the only concern is the honor of Christ, and the salvation of believers.

Thus would the case be easily understood, and thus might Paul's conduct serve as a pattern for us, if it were merely a matter of personal variance and not a strife respecting the nature of the doctrine itself. But, as we have already seen, this was by no means the case. It is a false form of doctrine, placing itself in competition with the preaching of Paul and in opposition to it, a mutilated and corrupted Gospel that is here spoken of. Those opposers, it is true, acknowledged Jesus to be the Christ, but not in the sense in which Paul received him. It was not in his full character as the sole ground of salvation, the central point of the whole Christian life, as he was regarded by Paul. Hence, we might naturally suppose, Paul could not rejoice that Christ was preached through them, since it was not in his pure complete character. And indeed, we see Paul dealing elsewhere quite differently with such persons. How

indignantly does he combat them in the Epistle to
the Galatians! He does not acknowledge them
as preachers of the same Gospel; he declares that
there is no other Gospel than that preached by
him; that they do but pervert the Gospel of
Christ. In opposition to those who would connect
with the Gospel the righteousness of the law, he
says: "If righteousness come by the Law, then
has Christ died in vain" (Gal. ii. 21). And in this
Epistle also he expresses himself, as we shall see
hereafter, with equal severity in regard to this
false tendency. How then is Paul's manner of
speaking in this passage, to be reconciled with
what he says in those other cases? It is only necessary to discriminate carefully the different relations, presupposed by this diversity of judgment
and conduct. Paul manifests this warmth of dis-
pleasure, only in cases where the Gospel had already gained a foothold among the Gentiles, and
where that judaizing tendency threatened to pervert it, by intermingling so much of Judaism as
wholly to obscure its peculiar nature. For it could
only cause him grief, that the blessing of which a
people were already in full possession, should be
marred and taken from them. But it was other-

wise here, where he speaks in relation to the
heathen who as yet knew nothing of Christianity.
Those preachers bore witness at least to the fact,
that Jesus had appeared to found the kingdom of
God in man; they testified of his history, the facts
of his life, his resurrection, his ascension to heaven;
although they did not themselves comprehend,
nor were able to unfold to others, how much was
involved in all this. Now Paul could not but rejoice that the common foundation of the Gospel,
a knowledge of the person and history of Christ,
should be made known to those who as yet had
heard nothing of them. This was the first thing;
the starting-point from which all the rest must
proceed. If this personage, these facts, became
once known and could be made objects of attention, here was a basis for still further labors. If
Christ, the crucified, the risen, the ascended Christ,
could but once be known and acknowledged,
those who had gone thus far might, from this
starting-point, be led onward to find still more in
him; might be assisted to search deeper and
deeper into the inexhaustible riches which are in
Christ. Paul could therefore rejoice that Christ
was preached, even though it was in this defective

manner; though the doctrine of Christ were not presented in its purity and completeness. There are, it must be remembered, different degrees in the knowledge of Christ. More or less may be found in him. We must therefore deal with no one as an enemy, because he has at first but little; but must help him on from this point that he may gain more, that he may become conscious of those greater treasures, which he needs but rightly to develop out of that which he has already received; "till," as Paul expresses it in the fourth chapter of the Epistle to the Ephesians, "we all come to the unity of the faith and of the knowledge of the Son of God, unto a perfect man, unto the measure of the stature of the fulness of Christ." Paul's conduct, in this case, is in accordance with the principle indicated by Christ himself. When the disciples met with one, who attributed to Christ's name a power whereby evil spirits might be cast out, they refused to allow the use of that name by one who had not as yet become his professed disciple, and who had not made common cause with them by uniting himself to their company. But Christ rebuked them, in those memorable words: "He who is not against us, is on

our part." "Not to be *against* Christ" contained
n itself the germ, from which the positive, "to be
for Christ," might yet be developed.   Though he
did not as yet know Christ as the Apostles knew
him, though he was still ignorant of the true sig-
nificance and power of this name, and connected
many errors with his belief in its efficacy; still it
was a germ of faith not to be despised, a germ from
which more might develope itself and be developed.   It was a point of connection, from which one
who had gained so much could be led still farther.
It needed only that he should be brought to perceive what was implied in this, what must be pre-
supposed in the strange efficacy of the invocation
of Christ's name.   Who must HE be, from whose
name such power proceeds!   In what relation
must He stand to the kingdom of evil, when his
name exercises such sway over evil spirits!   It is
clear that he who had once acknowledged so much
was already in a position, from which, with patience and love, he might be conducted farther
and farther in knowledge and faith.   From him
who as yet was only not an opposer of Christ, who
knew and recognized Christ in some single point
of view, might be formed by building upon that

which he had already attained, a positive disciple
of Christ. But he might also, if not thus dealt
with, if too much was required of him with his
present attainments, be wholly repelled. Not
only might he be hindered from farther progress
by such harsh treatment, but be unsettled in regard to what he had already gained; and thus the
germ of truth, in its yet imperfect development,
might be wholly destroyed. Against such a
course we are warned by those words of Christ;
and with these Paul accords when he rejoices that
Christ was preached and acknowledged, even
though in an obscured and defective manner.

We have already, before we saw clearly the
relation which these opposers held to Paul, and
regarding them merely in general as his personal
enemies, felt ourselves constrained to acknowledge
him as a model of self-denying zeal for the cause
of Christ. We are now, after a more full and
careful development of this relation, called upon
to contemplate this great model under a new light.
It implies a love purified from selfishness far
above what is common, to be able to recognize and
with joy to acknowledge the work of the Lord,
when performed through the agency of a personal

enemy. But the power of this purified and exalted love reveals itself under still another view,
when the truth lying at the basis of even an erroneous representation of the Gospel is recognized
and welcomed; when the seed of truth is not re-
jected and spurned on account of the error, even
though this may oppose itself to a purer, more
complete, unmutilated conception of the Gospel as
preached by ourselves, but is welcomed as one
step towards the farther advancement of the Gospel. But how seldom do we find a like example!
One who is capable, it may be, of joyfully wel-
coming the work of the Lord when advanced by
means of a personal enemy, might yet not be able
so far to forget self as to accept with cordial love,
and to use for the common cause of the Lord, the
truth lying at the bottom of the errors promulga-
ted by his opponent, especially when in direct
opposition to the pure truth which he is himself
conscious of preaching. How different would it
have been in the church, how many divisions
might have been avoided, how many who have labored only to oppose each other might have labored together for the spread of the Gospel;
how many who have hardened themselves in their

errors, and have lost by degrees even so much of
divine truth as they had embraced, might from
that partial view have been led farther and farther
in the knowledge of the truth, and have been
gradually made free from the bondage of error;
if Christians, instead of demanding everything at
once, with the impatient zeal of a love not suffi-
ciently purified from self, had been more observ-
ant of the various grades of faith and knowledge,
and had nurtured them with a forbearing charity!

The principle here expressed and acted on by
Paul admits of numerous applications. But to
what form of Christian labor is the immediate
reference here? To that which most exactly corresponds to Paul's peculiar vocation, that where
the first concern is to establish the church upon
the one foundation, which is Christ; we mean the
missionary work. Here should all, after Paul's
example, fix their aim upon this single point, to
make CHRIST everywhere known, to testify only
of Him. Here, then, should the strife respecting
differences in the form of representation and differences of creed find no place; and amidst all
diversities on these points, there should be a union
of labor for the one object of proclaiming Christ.

Whatever differences may exist on other points, should all be made an offering to his cause. To each one it should be matter of rejoicing that through others also, and even such as in his view have a less perfect knowledge of Christ, He, the great centre of all, is made more and more widely known. We may apply this example of Paul in still another view. There are times in which the church, even where it is already firmly established, is called on to exercise anew a missionary activity; times in which the ideas and tendencies to which Christianity first gave being and currency, though still exerting their influence upon society, yet deny their connection with Christianity, and even array themselves against it. Such are times of wide-wasting apostasy; when the culture, which has grown up under the fostering care of Christianity, rises up in opposition to it,—an opposition which may, however, have been first called forth by the impure mixture of human institutions with Christianity. Such periods occur in the history of all religions, when reason, matured to self-dependence, disunites itself from the faith under whose guardianship it has been nurtured. Nor could Christianity escape this fate.

It is subject to the same laws and conditions as all things human; and distinguishes itself only in the manner in which, by virtue of its divine nature and character, it rises victorious from all such con flicts. For whilst other religions find in such conflicts their grave, to Christianity they prove but the transition points to a resurrection, in increased purity and glory, in the energy of a renewed youth. In such times, as well as in periods of missionary labor, does the principle "that CHRIST alone be preached" find anew its application. The sole concern then is, that Christ should first of all be brought near to the souls estranged from him, that he may draw them to himself and make them subject to him. Here too, all cannot be achieved at once; but gradually, from the common relation to the one Christ, must the way be opened for a union among souls reclaimed to him from the most diverse forms of error. Here must Paul's example of magnanimous denial of self be our guide. Here every one, who is animated by the same spirit with the Apostle, must rejoice if "in every way CHRIST is preached," even when he cannot but feel that the manner leaves much to be desired.

Still another trait of Paul's Christian character

is presented to us, in his manner of accepting the
gifts sent to him by the Philippian church. There
is in the natural man a false striving after independence and self-reliance; a pride of self-will,
which not seldom decks itself with noble names,
the influence of which is to make one ashamed to
accept from others gifts of which he stands in
need, lest he should humble himself before them.
A still worse development of the same radical
fault of the natural man is seen, when the gifts
indeed are accepted and enjoyed, but there is a
disposition to forget them again, to shun the re-
membrance of them, to acknowledge no indebted-
ness to others through fear of seeming dependent,
of humbling one's self before them. But the
Apostle is penetrated by the consciousness, that
all are related to each other as the members of
one body, and should abide in this mutual dependence upon one another as members under one
head, Christ Jesus. He knows that the growth
of the whole body, from the one head which
guides animates and connects all the members,
can only then be truly promoted, when all the
single members are ready, as instruments of the
one head, mutually to sustain and forward each

other in spiritual and in temporal things, to work together in love and unity. This is beautifully expressed by Paul in the Epistle to the Ephesians (iv. 15, 16): "That we grow up into him in all things, which is the head, even Christ; from whom the whole body fitly joined together, and compacted by that which every joint supplieth, according to the effectual working in the measure of every part, maketh increase of the body unto the edifying of itself in love." Christ is here presented as the one to whom the whole development must tend; the aim of all is to grow up into true fellowship with him, to receive him wholly into themselves, to become full of him. He is equally the one, from whom the whole growth up into him can alone proceed; from whom issue all the vital energies, the living juices; from whom alone all the members can receive life and direction. Christ so works upon the whole body, that by means of the different members through which his vitalizing influence flows, using each in its appropriate manner, he works through the whole. And hence the growth, proceeding from him and tending up to him, can truly prosper only when all the members alike yield themselves to him; and under his guidance, in mutual dependence and mutual influence upon each other, abide together in closest union. The Christian should ever bear in mind, that our various necessities, and the means of supplying them, are distributed in varying modes and proportions through the different members, in order to keep them in a state of mutual dependence and reciprocal influence; so that no one may break loose from his connection with the whole, thinking to maintain an existence by himself, and that mutual necessities may serve continually for the furtherance of mutual love. The Christian will not be ashamed, therefore, of a dependence upon others springing from such a connection; but will recognize it as the law naturally arising from the relation of the members to one another. As he who gives rejoices in having received from God means which he may use for the aid of the other members; regarding it as a loan for this purpose from their common Lord, as a medium for the manifestation of that love which the Spirit of God has poured into the hearts of believers, that being the mark by which the disciples of the Lord, the members of his body, are to be known : so he that

receives rejoices far less in the brief temporal service of the gift, than in the heavenly temper expressed in the bestowal,—in the love, that vital
principle of the church, which manifests itself therein. He knows that it is for the highest good of the
giver himself; who thus, by deeds of love, sows
in the earthly life what he shall reap in life eternal; who thus manifests in his works the spirit
which makes him meet for life eternal. So Paul
represents the Christian relation, in his own manner of accepting the gifts of the Philippian
church, when he says: "I rejoiced in the Lord
greatly that now at length your care for me hath
flourished again,"—rejoiced, that now after long-
endured privation, they are placed once more in a
condition to fulfil the wish they had ever felt, to
care for his temporal wants;—" because ye have
ever cared for me, but ye lacked opportunity.
Not that I speak in respect of want." And in
conclusion he says: "Not because I desire a gift,
but I desire fruit"—the fruit which springs for
them out of such manifestations of love—"which
may abound to your account"—may be laid up for
life eternal.

Again: Paul here gives us a model of the genuine Christian character, in his demeanor in respect to external things. The Christian, in the power of the Lord through which he is able to do all things, proves his independence of the world, and his supremacy over it, by his ability to endure joyfully all the privations which the Lord lays upon him, in the circumstances of his lot, in what is required of him by his calling. His soul, filled with the divine life, cannot be bowed down by earthly want. Subjected to privation, he so much the more feels and proves his inward mastery of the world. But the Christian is far also from that self-imposed mortification of the flesh, in an imaginary spirituality, which nevertheless only serves for the satisfaction of the fleshly mind; for in the Holy Scriptures, all which does not proceed from the divine Spirit, all which comes from our own will, therefore every form of vanity and spiritual pride is ascribed to the flesh. (Coloss. ii. 23.*) He is far from imposing upon himself privations, in order thereby to merit any-

---

* This passage, incorrectly translated by Luther, stands thus in the original: "which (namely, the principles spoken of in vss. 21 and 22) have indeed a show of wisdom in self-chosen spirituality and humility and mortification of the body, but have no worth, serving only for the satisfying of the flesh." Ex. MSS.

thing before God or man, though submitting joy-fully to those which God lays upon him; but accepts with humble gratitude whatever God may bestow upon him above what is required for his absolute wants. The Christian's greatness is ever built upon humility. His independence of the world, his supremacy over it, consists in just this, that in every condition of want or abundance he is the same, neither depressed by want nor seduced by prosperity into worldliness and vain-glory; that he uses both alike in order to make known that divine life by which he is raised above the world. This is the spirit which Paul here exhibits when he says, that though he needs not the Philippians' gifts of love, he still rejoices in that love which prompted them; and when to this he adds the testimony, that he has accustomed himself to all changes of condition; that he knows how to adapt himself equally to all circumstances, whether of want or abundance, through the power of Him who animates him. "I have learned," says he, "in whatsoever state I am, therewith to be content. I know both how to be abased, and I know how to abound; in every respect and in all things I am fully instructed, both to be full and to be hungry, both to abound and to suffer need. I can do all things through Christ which strengtheneth me." Such is true Christian fortitude and greatness of soul, whose basis is humility.

SECTION SECOND.

AFTER having thus carefully considered Paul in his then existing circumstances and temper of mind, let us now turn our attention to the state of the Philippian church, and to what Paul has to say in reference to this, by way of warning and counsel for the future.

We will first take a general view, and from this pass to particulars.

It is customary with Paul to commence his letters, with a recognition of whatever is praiseworthy in the church to which he is writing. In this appears his wisdom as a spiritual guide. The confidence of men is far more easily won, and a hearing secured for whatever one has to say in the way of admonition and rebuke, if it appears that he nowise overlooks or undervalues what is good in them, that he does not willingly find fault, but is ready to acknowledge every real excellence with cordial approbation. Good and bad, more-

over, stand frequently in close connection with each
other.   The good lies at the foundation ; but the
evil mingles its disturbing influence with the good,
and hence it is through the latter that we can best
reach and remedy the former.   It is in the clear
perception of this relation, and in the skilful use of it
for the correction of error, that Paul manifests his
wisdom.   Of this a striking example is furnished in
the first epistle to the Corinthians.   Thus Paul regards whatever of real value he finds already existing in the churches, not as something produced
in them from themselves and by their own agency,
but wrought in them by the Spirit of God, that
Spirit which has begun to transform them into
new men.   Hence he feels himself constrained to
thank God for that which He has wrought in their
hearts and in their lives by his grace, before he of-
fers to Him the prayer, that what He has already
wrought in them He will more and more purify,
carry it forward, and bring it to perfection.   Upon
the good which already exists in them he builds the
hope, that they will ever continue to advance in
goodness, even unto perfection.   Not indeed upon
the good as a work of man can he rest such a hope.
He knows too well the weakness of man, too well

how subject is everything human to constant
change. But this is the ground of his hope, that
in this beginning of the Christian life he sees not
the work of man but the work of God. He thus
builds his hope upon the truth and faithfulness of
God, who will certainly carry forward what He
has begun, through all conflicts and trials, safely
to its consummation. It is not God's way to do
things by halves. Thus too does Paul begin his
letter to the Philippians ; thanking God for their
living fellowship in the gospel from the beginning
up to the present hour ; and then expressing the
confidence, that He who has begun in them the.
good work will also carry it on to its completion.
In this it is indeed always presupposed by Paul,
that they likewise will do what belongs to them,
by yielding themselves to the power of God which
works nothing without man, albeit man without it
can work nothing ; as in the eleventh chapter of
the epistle to the Romans (v. 22), he represents
the continued manifestation of God's goodness in
men as conditioned on their continuing in His
goodness, and thus susceptible of the grace of God
by truly yielding themselves up to its influence.
It is on this connection between the divine and the

human he founds the exhortation, " to work out
their salvation with fear and trembling; for," he
adds, " it is God who worketh in you both the
willing and the doing, of his own good pleasure." It
is here assumed that the salvation of man is conditioned upon his own conduct. He is himself to
work out his salvation. And yet Paul always
represents the salvation of man as something which
can be accomplished only through the grace of
God, as the work of God in man. But he adds, in
this passage, a more exact designation of the temper of heart with which they should work out
their salvation, viz., " with fear and trembling."
This would not be appropriate if he were speaking
of what lay merely in the hand of man, in which
case all would depend upon his own strength. It
is because Paul is conscious of the weakness and
insufficiency of all human strength, because he presupposes that man can do nothing without God,
and must constantly watch over himself, lest
through his own fault he lose the aid of divine
grace, without which all human efforts are in vain;
it is for this reason that he designates this temper
of mind as one of fear and trembling, as the feeling of personal accountability and helplessness, of

insecurity and instability in ourselves, by which we may be ever admonished to continual watchfulness, and to ever-renewed waiting upon God as the fountain of all our strength. Hence, as the ground of such an admonition, he appeals to this consciousness that we can of ourselves do nothing, that it is God who alone bestows upon us the power to will and to perform what is needful to our salvation; that all, indeed, depends upon his sovereign will. This feeling of dependence, the ground-tone of the Christian life, is ever to be maintained. It is this which must combat the presumption of a vain human self-reliance, which, finding itself deceived in the result, so easily gives place to dejection and despair.

All the admonitions which Paul gives the Philippians in reference to the Christian walk, are comprehended in this one; that they should "walk in a manner worthy of the Gospel of Christ." And what is required of them in their position, in the midst of a corrupt world, he points out in chapter ii. 15–16. Inasmuch, he says, as they are called to live as children of God in the midst of a corrupt world, they are called to maintain unsullied, amidst all the defilements of surrounding pollution, that divine life of which, as children of God, they have become participants, and to show forth its glory in contrast with the perverse generation in which they live. The terms "crooked and perverse," in which Paul describes this wicked generation, have reference to the perversion of the original godlike nature, which can be restored only through the new creation. So also, as children of God, they are to shine as lights, as radiant luminaries in the world of darkness. Whilst all around them is darkness, here alone shall all be light. So indeed does Christ say to those who belong to his kingdom, that they are to be the lights of the world, just as He is the Sun who sends his light into this dark world, its light in the highest and only true sense. Thus what He is, is communicated to those who enter into fellowship with him, and they too through him become the light of the world. This light shines in the holy walk of Christians, and thereby do they testify of Him who is light itself, and in whom is no darkness; thereby do they glorify him and lead others to acknowledge and honor him; as Christ himself has said: "Let your light so shine before men, that they seeing your good works may glorify your

Father which is in Heaven." They are to testify
of that which is life, to show forth the true life in
this world of death.* Everything which men, in
accordance with the revelation of the law written
in their consciences through the impulses of their
moral nature, are accustomed to account moral and
virtuous, belongs also to the peculiar stamp of this
new divine life, in which the children of God manifest themselves as such. All must find its fulfilment here; only that is done away which proceeds
from the disturbing influence of sin; as Christ says,
that he " came not to destroy but to fulfil." Hence
it is the conclusion of Paul's exhortation,† that
their minds be directed only to "what is true"—
(true and good being in the biblical sense one and
the same, the truth here appears as that which
penetrates and gives direction to the whole life;
all has its root in the truth, the true is the divine)
—to "what is becoming, what is upright, what is
chaste, what is lovely, what is of good report, whatever is virtue and whatever is praise." Thus it is
implied by Paul, that the divine life must manifest
itself in an amiable form before men; and he ap-

---

* As in some MSS. " holding forth the true life."
† Chap. iv. 8.

peals to what they had learned from his instructions, and had witnessed in the example of his own
life. Although, as we have seen above, he was far
from holding his life to be entirely pure and perfect, yet he could with confidence assume the essential correspondence between his life and teachings,
and that his conduct did not give the lie to his instructions. And thus he was able, without un-
truth or self-exaltation, to hold up to the Philippians the example of his own course among them
as an admonition to them. Self-exaltation is the
less to be attributed to him here, as he was himself fully conscious, that whatever in his own conduct he proposed as their example was only the
work of grace, the fruit of the new creation in him.
So may the Christian when made aware, by a comparison of his earlier and later life, of having gained
the victory over the old nature in any of its sinful
tendencies, be fully conscious of this and freely rejoice over it; for this is no self-exaltation. He
knows that it is not to his own nature or his own
strength that he is indebted for it; that the Spirit
of God, the Spirit of Christ has wrought this in
him; and therefore the consciousness of his victory
only impels him to praise and to thank Him, through

whose power he has attained it. And at the same time, he feels himself constrained to acknowledge how much still remains for him to contend with, and with the Apostle, whose words we have quoted, to forget what is behind and press continually forward.

The church at Philippi, as we have already remarked, had been called to endure many forms of persecution. It was necessary that Paul should exhort them to steadfastness under these trials. How then does he express himself? It is important for us to bring this out clearly, for it is applicable to all the conflicts which Christianity has to encounter in all times. They should in no wise suffer themselves to be terrified by their adversaries;* "which to them is an evident token of perdition, but to you of salvation and that of God. For to you it is given, for the sake of Christ—not only to believe on him—but for his sake to suffer also." What is the full import of these words? This is best shown by contrast. Had the opposers of the gospel succeeded in terrifying the Philippians, it would thereby have been made manifest how much these opposers could effect, what power

* Chap. i. 28, 29.

they possessed; the weakness of the Philippians would have appeared, and the cause which they served might have seemed an impotent one. Or it might have seemed merely a contest between man and man, their opponents being the stronger and they the weaker party. Their demeanor would have been a testimony, how much was still wanting to them of that divine power which was to manifest its efficacy in believers; how much, therefore, they still lacked of the genuine life of faith. But while they did not suffer themselves to be terrified by those who warred with weapons of the flesh, this was a proof that they were in the service of a divine cause, victorious over all human opposition; that a power of God wrought in them against which no human force could avail. The conflict with their adversaries served but to test and to approve their faith, and their power through faith. It was a proof of the vanity of their opposers' efforts; even as Christ reckons it as one of the works of the Holy Spirit, to lead men to the conviction that the Prince of this world has been judged, and hence can accomplish nothing farther through his instruments (Jno. xvi. 11). Thus through them is this power of the Holy Spirit manifested. So far, it

was an evidence of the condemnation drawn upon
themselves by those who warred in the service of
the Prince of this world. But for the Philippians,
it was for that very reason a certain proof, a pledge,
of their salvation; for the faith which remains
steadfast in conflict is indeed assured of salvation. It was the pledge that the power of God,
through which they were able to hold themselves
unterrified by their adversaries, would also lead
them through all conflicts to final salvation; as in
the works of God one thing answers to another, one
guaranties the other. And thus Paul gives special prominence to the thought, that this is not of
man; that it is no illusive human proof, but a factual proof given by God himself. It is one part
of this proof, that to them it was given of God to
suffer for Christ's sake. For whoever follows
Christ in his sufferings, must needs follow him also
in his glorification. Paul had said, " for Christ's
sake;" intending at first only to say, " for Christ's
sake to suffer." But he would bring out the full
meaning of this with a stronger emphasis. He
therefore interrupts himself, and says, " not merely
to believe on him, but for his sake to suffer also."
He who believes in Christ is, so far as his faith ap-

proves itself to be genuine, certain of the blesset·
ness of heaven. But it is also requisite that this
faith approve itself to be genuine, by assuring its
possessors against all fear of their adversaries; and
by giving them the power to follow Christ in his
sufferings, as in general its office is, in all things, to
bring them into fellowship with Christ. And
therefore, although with faith in Christ, as the root
of all else pertaining to the Christian life, all else
is given so far as regards the principle whence it
springs, the germinating power which produces it;
yet to suffer for Christ is more than merely to believe
on him, inasmuch as through these sufferings
the power of faith makes itself manifest, approves
itself to be genuine. For one might suppose himself
the possessor of that genuine faith, and yet the
result, when he was found to shun a participation
in the sufferings of Christ, would prove the contrary.
In another view, indeed, suffering is of less
account than faith. For there might be a suffering
too, which was not true Christian suffering, as not
proceeding from the life of faith, that faith which
works by love. As Paul says in 1 Cor. xiii. 3;
"And though I give my body to be burned, and
have not charity, it profiteth me nothing." The

same is true, in general, of the relation of faith to
the entire course of Christian life in its outward
manifestation, of the relation of faith to good works.
It everywhere finds an application, in a greater or
less degree, in respect to the relation of the inward
to the outward, of the internal feeling to its manifestation in action.

The Christian life is no instinctive, unconscious
one. It follows not feeling alone; but demands,
everywhere and in all things, an intelligent discrimination between what is of God and what is
not, in respect to all the relations of life; between
what accords to the will of the Lord, to the spirit·
and nature of Christianity, and what is in contrariety thereto. It cannot subsist, cannot fulfil its
mission, without a considerate conscious process of
scrutiny and discrimination. As flesh and spirit
are still coexisting in the Christian, and are ever in
conflict with each other; so the power of discriminating what proceeds from the one or the other,
what is in accordance with the one or the other, is
continually needed, in order that the Christian
may not yield to the suggestions of the flesh, when
he thinks he is acting according to the impulses of
the spirit. Of such a testing and discriminating

process there was especial need, in churches established in the midst of the Pagan or Jewish world;
since there, Christianity, contending with existing
customs relations and views of life which were the
product of another spirit and principle, was now
first to bring into existence a new creation, in which
Christ should be all in all. Here of course the
question must often arise : What does Christianity
require ? In what respects does the heathen or
Jewish point of view stand opposed to it ? Wherein may the Christian conform himself to the world,
wherein may he not ? For this reason Paul, in his
practical admonitions to this church, desires for
them especially increase in knowledge,* in the faculty of perception; that they might test things
which differ, the good and the bad, the true and
the false, that thus they might avoid the one and
choose the other. Paul assumes that, for this work,
the diligent exercise of the faculty of perception is
necessary; that such a power of discernment is the
fruit of unremitting exercise of the Christian judgment. In like manner in the epistle to the He-
brews (v. 14), it is accounted one of the attributes
of the state of Christian maturity, that, through

* Chap. i. 9.

the exercise of the organs of spiritual perception,
a readiness had been attained for distinguishing
good and evil. But if, on the one hand, there are
objects of knowledge and judgment where all de
pends on the exercise of the understanding, where
he who is most practised in thinking possesses also
the best judgment, and is most fully guarded
against error; yet in regard to the objects which
the Apostle has in mind, those pertaining to moral
duties, this is by no means the case. In general,
we shall often find how much the judgment is here
biassed by the direction of the will. The mistakes
which lie at the basis of action, and errors in conduct, arise not so much from defect in the thinking
faculty, as from selfish inclinations which sway the
judgment. And this is particularly the case with
Christianity, which assigns wholly new objects as
the aim of life. To know what is in harmony with
it, LOVE must be the controlling and directing principle of the whole life. The more entirely one is
animated by love, the more will his moral judgment be in harmony with Christianity. A soul,
however well practised in thinking, will miss the
right, if not thus quickened and the eye of the
spirit made single by love. To this we must add,

that Christianity is no mere law of the letter,
which establishes only single general rules of duty,
according to which all single cases of conduct are
to be determined; but it is a law of the Spirit,
which makes known to each individual his peculiar
mission in life, that very one which the Lord has
appointed him to fulfil, and what is needed for its
fulfilment.   No one can prescribe to another, what
from his standpoint, under his appointed relations,
it is his duty to do; but it is LOVE, that spirit
common to all, which makes known to each in
particular what is duty for him, and in reference
to this leads him to make the necessary discrimination.   To love, therefore, Paul here gives the first
place, and ascribes to its quickening presence the
knowledge and capacity required for distinguishing
the good and the bad, the true and the false ; as
he himself expresses it, " that your love may more
and more abound in all knowledge;" meaning,
that *therein* its effect is seen,—that increase of
knowledge in the fruit of more abundant love.
But as here the theoretical proceeds from the
practical, the new direction of the judgment from
the new direction of the will, of the moral disposition; so is the theoretical in like manner to react .

upon the practical, the enlightened judgment upon
the conduct. Hence Paul adds, as the object to be
thus attained, that they should continue " pure and
irreproachable" in their Christian walk, until all
shall appear before the Lord ; " being filled with
the fruit of righteousness, which is by Jesus Christ,
to the glory and praise of God." Thus Paul here
designates righteousness, not as something to be
gradually acquired ; but on the contrary, it is pre-
supposed as something inherent in their fellowship
with Christ, flowing out to them from him, as produced in them by his Spirit. He contemplates the
entire Christian life as the fruit of this righteousness; not speaking, as in other passages, of single
fruits in single works, but of the whole Christian
course in its connected unity as one fruit, and that
the fruit which is produced by Jesus Christ. That
from him all proceeds, that through him all is accomplished, is the very thing which gives to such
a life its peculiar stamp. This it is which is truly
well-pleasing unto God, and by which God is truly
glorified, even as the whole life of Christ was a
glorifying of God in our nature. But it is also
clear from what has been said, that though, as a
whole, the Christian life is thus represented as a

fruit of righteousness produced by Jesus Christ,
yet with this are presupposed many different stages
of development, many separate results of the reciprocal working of the practical and theoretical, of
the moral disposition and the judgment, as necessary to the production of this sum total; just as
the fruit of the tree, to follow the image chosen by
Paul, does not attain to its full form and maturity
at once, but through many preparatory stages in
the natural process of development and growth.

We have already observed Paul's manner of
contemplating the church as a whole consisting
of various members, whose growth is dependent
on the harmonious co-operation of all. But many
hindrances stood opposed to this harmonious action; and these could only be overcome gradually by the subduing power of the Christian spirit.
Only by degrees, and through the power of that
spirit, could this higher unity be formed out of
the conflicting elements, existing in the church.
Some of these originated in national differences, in
the modes of thought peculiar to those of Jewish
or of pagan parentage. From these arose those
opposite leading tendencies, of which we shall
speak more particularly hereafter. There was also

the difference of rank and wealth, which threatened to impair the spirit of oneness and equality in the Christian body. And, finally, there were differences arising from peculiarities in constitution and mental endowments, all which had been brought by Christianity into its service. Hence the diversities in the operations of the Holy Spirit, animating these different natural gifts; and hence too the diversity of spiritual gifts, and of offices connected with them, in the church. From all these diversities collisions might arise, disturbing the unity and harmony of the church; each might wish to magnify what was peculiar to himself, and thus self-exaltation and disunion follow, occasioning strife among the members. Here then, in order to secure that unity in the church which belongs to its nature, all must be harmonized by the victorious spirit of love. It is clear how important and necessary, under these relations, were Paul's reproofs and admonitions, his warnings against self-exaltation and disunion, his exhortations to humility and harmony. Let us examine this point more particularly. If they would make his joy complete,* they must be of the same mind,

* Chap. ii. 2, 3.

having the same love, being of one accord, of one
mind; nothing must be done through party spirit
or vain ambition, but in humility each must esteem others better than himself. But how are we
to understand this? One's judgment of another
is not within the control of his own will. How
can he esteem his brother higher than himself, if
this is not in accordance with the truth; if he cannot but perceive in himself excellencies which are
wanting to the other, and defects in the other from
which he is himself free? How can it be required
of him to do violence to his judgment? Is he to
practise deception upon himself? Is humility to
be grounded upon falsehood? Most certainly not.
If one should endeavor to work himself into such
a judgment of others in comparison with himself,
or should express such a judgment without really thinking so, this would be mere hypocrisy in
a grosser or more refined form. But there is here
pre-supposed, as resulting from the full development of the Christian life, a pervading temper of
heart, of which such a judgment of one's self in
comparison with others is but the necessary and
natural expression. The Christian's love will lead
him first of all to discern what is good in another,

to discover even in his blemishes his peculiar gifts,
that in which he is really superior to himself;
while, on the other hand, through a self-scrutiny
sharpened by the Spirit which quickens him, he
detects with rigorous exactness his own faults.
And this self-rigor, united with love, will give
leniency to his judgment of whatever may obscure
the divine life in others. Thus a readiness to take
such a position, in respect to others, as is here represented, will not be a mere casual thing with
the Christian, something produced in him from
without by external influence; but is the sponta-
neous result of the internal process of Christian
development. And this manner of viewing one's
self, in relation to others, will appear likewise in
his whole conduct in regard to them. The idea is
of course excluded that one should make himself
the centre of all, referring everything to himself,
and thus regarding all others as existing but for
him. It is clear how greatly others will in this
way rise in his estimation. This spirit of love and
humility will manifest itself in his deportment
towards others; and hence it is added: "Look not
each one upon his own things, but also on the
things of others." Let each one be ready to sub-

ordinate his own interest to that of others, to deny
himself for the welfare of others. Paul says,
"also," although the form of the first clause would
not lead us to expect such a limitation. But he
adds this "also" because it is not his aim wholly
to exclude the care for our own interests, but only
to oppose the tendency to make this predominant,
to allow it to swallow up all else. Of course he
here speaks only of human, worldly interests,
which one is bound to sacrifice for the best good
of others; for in regard to that which is the highest and properly real interest of each one personally, his own soul's welfare, the cultivation of the
inner man for the life of eternity, no such contrariety can exist, no such requirement of self-denial
can be made. But does this seem to conflict with
what we have previously remarked of self-denial
in reference even to the higher interests of the
spirit? By no means. The true, the highest interest of the spirit, that it should be ever growing in self-denying love, in purification from all
selfishness, thereby becoming ever more meet for
the kingdom of God and eternal life, this must always be promoted by such sacrifices, even in reference to what we call the higher interests of the

soul, which yet are not its highest interest. In reference to such a temper and course of conduct, Paul now presents, as the type and pattern, Him after whom the whole Christian life in its spirit and conduct should be moulded, CHRIST HIMSELF. " Let the same mind be in you which was also in Christ Jesus: who, being in the form of God, did not eagerly claim equality with God;* (so, we think the Greek is more truly expressed than in Luther's version;) but emptied himself, taking the form of a servant, being made in the likeness of men; and being found in fashion as a man, he humbled himself, becoming obedient unto death, even the death of the cross. Therefore also hath God exalted him over all, and hath given him a name which is above every name, that in the name of Jesus every knee should bow, of beings in heaven and upon the earth and underneath the earth, and every tongue confess that Jesus Christ is Lord to the glory of God the Father."

That we may rightly understand the use here made of the example of Christ, as the model after which the Christian life is to be formed, we must

---

* In his appearance on earth, as understood by Neander; see page 103, line 3.—TR.

first endeavor to bring the model itself clearly and distinctly before our minds. Before the eye of the Apostle stands the image of THE WHOLE CHRIST, the Son of God appearing in the flesh, manifesting himself in human nature. From the human manifestation he rises to the Eternal Word (as John expresses it), that Word which was, before the appearance of the Son of God in time, yea, before the worlds were made; in whom before all time God beheld and imaged hinself; as Paul in the Epistle to the Colossians calls him, in this view, the image of the invisible, i. e. of the incomprehensible God. Then, after this upward glance of his spiritual eye, he descends again into the depths of the human life, in which the Eternal Word appears as man. He expresses this in the language of immediate perception, beholding the divine and human as one; not in the form of abstract truth, attained by a mental analysis of the direct object of thought. Thus he contemplates the entrance of the Son of God into the form of humanity as a self-abasement, a self-renunciation, for the salvation of those whose low estate he stooped to share. He whose state of being was divine, who was exalted above all the wants and limitations of the finite and earthly existence, did not eagerly claim this equality with God which he possessed; but, on the contrary, he concealed and disowned it in human abasement, and in the forms of human dependence. And as the whole human life of Christ proceeded from such an act of self-renunciation and self-abasement, so did his whole earthly life correspond to this one act even to his death; the consciousness on the one hand of divine dignity which it was in his power to claim, and on the other the concealment, the renunciation of this, in every form of humiliation and dependence belonging to the earthly life of man. The crowning point appears in his death,—the ignominious and agonizing death of the cross. Paul now proceeds to show what Christ attained by such self-renunciation, thus carried to the utmost limit, by such submissive obedience in the form of a servant; the reward which he received in return, the dignity which was conferred upon him.

Here too is presented the universal law, laid down by Christ himself, that whoso humbles himself, and in proportion as he humbles himself, shall be exalted. Now it is of itself apparent that He who, according to Paul's teaching, was in his own

nature elevated above all, the first-born over the
whole creation, He through whom and in whom
all was created, could not as such be exalted.
But, as already intimated, it is the image of the
One Christ uniting in himself the divine and human, which is here before the mind of Paul.   Of
this Christ in humanity it might be predicated,
that He is as man exalted above all,—the glorified
Son of man.   And this his exaltation subserves no
selfish interest.   He finds his exaltation in the salvation of fallen beings.   This was its end, in this
indeed it should consist, that by the universal acknowledgment of Him as Lord and Saviour and
subjection to Him as such, God might be glorified
in Him and through Him; glorified in the triumphant establishment of his kingdom.   What application then is to be made of this example, in the
connection in which the Apostle introduces it?
As Christ aimed only to subserve the salvation of
men, so should Christians be ready to labor thus
for the salvation of their brethren. . As Christ offered up all for the salvation of men, so should
Christians also be ready to offer up all for the salvation of their brethren; to give up everything
for others, in order to secure their highest welfare;

thus in self-humiliation and self-renunciation following their Lord. So shall the life of the Christian too, from its first spiritual beginning, from the first act of faith, be a continuous self-abasement and self-renunciation. And this being the ground and condition of Christ's exaltation as the Son of man, so shall the same be, for believers who thus follow Christ, the ground and condition of their exaltation, till they come to share the full glory of Him whom they follow. We may compare this with a similar development of the same thought by Paul in 2 Cor. viii. 9, where he says of Christ: "Though he was rich, yet for our sakes he became poor." To the "being rich" corresponds the "being in divine form," the "being equal with God," in the passage before us; to the "becoming poor," the self-renunciation and self-abasement in the human servant-form, in its full extent as exhibited above. In the passage just quoted, this is used as an exhortation to that benevolence which sacrifices its own, subjects itself to privations, in order to relieve the necessities of others. It is based on the general thought, arising from a contemplation of the life of Christ, that each one should be ready to give up and to renounce all that he has for the

5*

highest good of others; the beneficent and conde
scending spirit of self-denying Christian love, which
pervades the whole Christian life in all its acts.
And in this general form is the thought conceived
in the passage before us.   It is this which charac-
terizes Paul as a moral teacher; that with him the
specific is in all cases carried back to the highest,
deepest, most comprehensive; that his special admonitions, in regard to the Christian life and character, have for their basis the general fundamental
ideas of the whole Christian life, all centering in
the example of Christ.

The church at Philippi needed the Apostle's admonitions and warnings, especially in reference to
the obstacles with which Christianity, in its process of development, then had chiefly to contend.
This process has in every age its peculiar obstacles
to overcome; and it would be easy to show a certain affinity between these opposing influences, although different periods give rise to different
forms.   But here an important distinction is to be
made.   There may be spiritual tendencies and
teachings, which come into direct conflict with the
peculiar essence of Christianity; a case where no
reconciliation is possible, but the choice must be

for the one or for the other; and where the decision for the pure Christian tendency, must manifest
itself in firm adherence to the one and steadfast
rejection of the other. Somewhat different is it
with those tendencies, which unite with the sincere
acknowledgment of Christian truth only a slight
remaining influence of former views, and which
form in their successive stages the gradual transition to pure Christian truth. This is especially
true of the obstacles, with which Christianity had
then to contend in its process of development. As
it was from Judaism the transition was made to
Christianity, so did the first important obstacle to
its process of development, arise from the inter-
mixture of views brought from the Jewish stand-
point. It is to these views that the distinction
above stated must be applied.

Such a predominance of the Jewish spirit did exist, through which the consciousness of the peculiar
nature of Christianity was essentially repressed and
stifled. Jesus was indeed outwardly acknowledged
as the Messiah; but there was wanting the true
import and power of such a conviction. He was
made, after the Jewish conception, a carnal Messiah with carnal hopes. As Christ, after the mir-

acle of the loaves, said to those who followed him with false views (John vi. 26), that it was not because they had seen the miraculous signs,—tokens of the manifestation of the divine in the world of sense, intended to point to a nature in itself divine made known through these tokens,—that not for these did they seek him, but because they had eaten of the loaves and were filled, that only sensual want attached them to him; so in these Jews of whom we are now speaking, there was the same lack of the divine sense, of the feeling of higher, inward, spiritual need. With them too it was only a mere sensual want, which led them to believe on Jesus. And though they differed from the Jews to whom Christ spoke in this respect, that they were not led by this similar fleshly tendency to open opposition against Jesus as the Messiah, but sought on the contrary to be outwardly united to him, yet no important advantage was thus gained. For while the former would not believe on a Jesus, who did not satisfy their physical necessities; the latter, believing in Jesus as the Messiah, yet made him nearly such an one as those had desired, and such as Jesus refused to be. With this one article, of faith in Jesus as the

Messiah in the sense here given, they united, as we have already seen, a strict adherence to the entire legal position. Not Jesus the Messiah was to them the sole ground of salvation; but in the observance of the whole Law, and in circumcision, they sought for righteousness and salvation. Not the righteousness which comes from within, from faith, was the object of their desire; but a righteousness which comes to man from without.

It is clear that where an opposition of this kind existed, there could be no agreement, no reconciliation. The true Christian spirit alone could make the decision, between a carnal or a spiritual Messiah; between a righteousness grounded on faith in the Redeemer alone, or in the Law and its works; between the transformation effected by the divine life, working from within the reformation of the whole man, or a mere external change in outward conduct; between God's work or man's work, humble acceptance of divine gifts, humble surrender to Jesus as the Saviour, or a carnal Messiah with the admission of the desert of one's own works. It was because the question for the new churches was of just such an unconditional opposition, between what was Christian and what was

unchristian, that Paul felt himself obliged to pre
sent the case so strongly, and to testify so earnestly
against those erroneous views. "Beware of dogs"
(the term in the original expressing the shameless
effrontery of these opposers of the truth); "beware of evil workers" (those who would supplant
the Christian by the Jewish stand-point); "beware of the concision." But how is it that Paul
here speaks of circumcision, which he nevertheless
regarded as a divine ordinance for a specific period,
in so contemptuous a manner? Circumcision was
in his estimation a divine seal, by which the theocratic people were separated, as the divinely consecrated race, from the nations abandoned to idol-
atry and its attendant abominations, for the purpose of conducting to that fellowship with God
which should one day embrace all humankind.
To him it was, as he says in the Epistle to the Romans, an outward symbol of the new relation to
God, into which Abraham entered by virtue of his
faith (Rom. iv. 11) ; and emblematical of that inward spiritual circumcision, the circumcision of
the heart in the spirit, of purification from the ex-
crescences of sin, which alone constitutes a true
people of God, through which alone the conception

of a people of God can find its realization. But
if now, as was the case with those Judaizers, justification and salvation were sought in this outward circumcision, as such; if indeed to faith in
Jesus as the Messiah, who in his true character
was the author of all righteousness, circumcision
was to be added as something higher, as the real
source of true righteousness; then was Paul bound
to expose, in the most emphatic manner, the utter
worthlessness of such an external act in reference
to the object to be attained. No words could
seem to him too strong to represent the perverse-
ness of such a view as this; which could ascribe
that to the external and sensuous, which can only
be produced from within, by virtue of what is
wrought within upon the spirit, through the im-
parting of a divine life. Hence he calls circumcision, in opposition to such an over-estimation of
it, a concision, a self-mutilation; and in the Epistle
to the Galatians, with a similar contemptuous al-
lusion to the abuse of this abrogated rite, he expresses the wish that those who made so much
account of circumcision would practise it to what
extent they pleased on themselves, provided they
would but leave other Christians in peace. Cer-

tainly that which seems to Paul as something so
unchristian and perverse, and excites in him so
much indignation, must have reference not merely
to circumcision, that single peculiarity of Judaism,
but to everything external and sensuous regarded
as a ground of justification, of sanctification, of
salvation; for, as such, it stands in direct opposition to that worship of God in spirit and in
truth, which springs solely from the inward act of
faith. This contrariety to the true Christian principle is expressed in the succeeding words, "For
we are the circumcision." That is, they are not
the truly circumcised, but their miscalled circumcision is a mere excision, a self-mutilation. We
are those who really deserve this name; we Christians are the truly circumcised; "we," he adds in
proof of the assertion, "who serve God in the
spirit, and glory in Christ Jesus, and have no confidence in the flesh." We must endeavor to develop the meaning of these weighty words. "To
serve God in the spirit," forms the direct opposite
to a worship of God connected with sensible, external, earthly things, and dependent thereon; a
worship which has not its spring in the spirit
within; as when one supposes that he can honor

God by receiving circumcision or by any external legal works, be they religious or moral, by any single acts whatever of external worship.

The true worship of God, on the contrary, Paul describes as one which proceeds from the spirit; meaning by this only such as can proceed from the renewing and sanctifying of the human spirit, by nature estranged from God, through the Holy Spirit which Christ alone imparts. Only thus can the spirit of man, being led back to fellowship with God and made a temple of God, become the sanctuary where God is worshipped aright; and then the whole life and conduct of the spirit is one act of divine worship. But as the redemption attained through Christ is here presupposed, as faith in the Redeemer and fellowship with him is the root and fountain of all, Paul therefore connects therewith the "glorying in the Lord;" i. e. glorying in such a manner as excludes all pride of human glory; a glorying in self-abasement; a glorying, to wit, only in Christ and in that which we are in him, which has its ground in him, for which we are indebted to him, and hence (what is but the counterpart of this) not placing our confidence in anything human. Paul presents his own case as an example in this respect to his Philippian brethren,—a proof of the sincerity of his teachings and admonitions. He appeals to the fact that he himself, as a born Jew brought up in the strictest Pharisaism, had lived in the exactest observance of the Law and yet had become convinced that all this could contribute nothing towards his cleansing from sin, his justification, sanctification and salvation; on which account he had renounced all this, in order to find all in Christ alone. He says that as respects the righteousness of the Law, he was blameless. This is said not merely of the requirements of the ceremonial law, but also of moral action so far as it meets the eye of man; both being comprehended under the term law. In all this Paul had been blameless. In the sight of men he was without blemish. What he says applies not less to what is called rectitude among men, than to a piety which consists in particular religious acts. Although Paul satisfied the claims which men could rightfully make on him, yet it availed him nothing. When, through the light of the Spirit, the true nature of the divine law and true self-knowledge dawned upon his mind, he seemed to himself, with

all this blamelessness before men, not less a sinner
on that account, wanting that true divine righteousness in which all flows out from God, and all
has reference to Him. HE is the true end and
aim of the whole life; while all that men call rectitude does not rise above the world. Hence he
says, implying the insufficiency of all this: "But
what things were gain to me, those I counted loss
for Christ. Yea, and I count all things but loss
for the excellency of the knowledge of Christ
Jesus my Lord: for whom I have suffered the loss
of all things, and do count them but dregs that I
may win Christ." He would say here, that everything which formerly was in his view a distinction,—as descent from the theocratic nation, legal
piety, blamelessness in a legal view,—all this now
appears to him a disadvantage, so far as he should
rest his confidence thereon and be thereby drawn
away from Christ. Christ having now become all
to him, all else must give place to Christ. All else,
high as it may be in itself, must appear loss if it
occasion the loss of Christ, whom none can gain but
those who seek and desire Him alone; for that very
knowledge of Christ, itself sufficing for all, in itself
comprehending all, outshines and eclipses all beside.

And hence Paul says, that for the sake of Christ he
has willingly suffered the loss of all; that he casts
all else away as worthless in order that he may win
Christ, who supplies to him the place of all. It is
his whole concern to be found in Christ,* to stand
in fellowship with him. And he thus contrasts
that divine righteousness, founded in this relation
and proceeding from inward faith, with a righteousness which comes from without, proceeding
from the works of the law, a merely human attainment secured by human efforts. In his view,
all here depends ON KNOWING CHRIST. This
knowledge is, in the Pauline sense, not something
merely intellectual, not a mere matter of specula-
tion, not certain specific articles of faith respecting
Christ as they are speculatively developed and
handed down; but, on the contrary, as shown in
the following words, it is a knowledge which takes
root in the life, a matter of personal experience,
the believer's inward perception of Christ as the
Son of God and his Redeemer. Paul then brings
forward into special prominence the power of his
resurrection, which of course presupposes the an-
nouncement of him as the Crucified, his sufferings

* Verse 9.

for the redemption of man from sin. This prominence he gives to the power of Christ's resurrection, as being the factual proof of the redemption effected by him;—as furnishing the evidence, in a glorified personality, of that imperishable divine life imparted to humanity, by virtue of the redemption from sin and consequent death; a life passing over from him to all who through faith stand in fellowship with him,—the beginning in them of a new divine life, to penetrate more and more their entire being, till they shall become wholly assimilated to it in soul and body. And hence he adds, "to know the fellowship of his sufferings;"—that is, how we are to follow him in sufferings, in order that we may more and more become partakers of the divine life in fellowship with the Risen One. He then sums up all in this, "to be made like unto him in his death;" to apply to one's self the image of his death, in order to attain to the fellowship of his resurrection. We must here refer back to what we have already said on this point, in another connection.* Thus we have here, in one view, all which pertains to the Christian life, all which constitutes the righteous-

* See p. 90.

ness of the Christian, in opposition to the requirements of legal piety or mere human rectitude.

The same class of persons is probably meant
when, in a subsequent passage,* after having proposed his own conduct as an example to the Philippians, he warns them with deep sorrow against
many who walk far otherwise, and whom he designates as enemies of the cross of Christ. Here,
however, the reference to this class of persons
cannot be proved with equal certainty. The
words "enemies of the cross of Christ" may be
applied to many classes of persons. They may be
understood of such as, indeed, acknowledge Jesus
the Crucified as their Saviour; but who still show
by their manner of thinking and acting, even
though themselves unconscious of it, that they are
enemies of the cross of Christ. It might be of
such as take their stand, consciously, as open enemies of the cross of Christ. This might at that
period proceed from two different points of view,
which indeed are found recurring in every age;
viz. from the position of the wisdom-seeking
Greeks, of whom Paul says that Jesus the Crucified
was to them foolishness, and from that of the sign-

* Verse 18.

seeking Jews, of whom he says that to them Jesus
the Crucified was an offence. It may be the unbelief which comes from the pride of wisdom,
from the pride of reason, from the pride of culture,
or the unbelief of the earthly sensual man. But
this open and conscious opposition cannot, as appears from the connection, be the one here meant.
It is inconsistent with the manner in which Paul
contrasts these enemies of the cross of Christ with
himself. Against such open opposers it was not
necessary thus to warn his brethren. The class
first mentioned must therefore be the one intended. Still the words admit of several applications.
This not open but rather unconscious enmity to
the cross of Christ, may be conceived as taking
either a practical or more theoretical form; as
manifesting itself only in action, or in doctrine as
well as in action. As respects the first, this again
may be understood in a two-fold manner. It may
mean such as are wanting in that humility, which
must spring from the belief that we owe all to the
cross of Christ, to Jesus who was crucified for us;
in whose life the conceit of self-righteousness, by
which the cross of Christ is disowned and disal-
lowed, predominates even though this may not

betray itself in the doctrines which they preach.
But it may also mean those who are far from
taking upon them their cross, and thus following
Jesus the Crucified; whose life, still devoted to
flesh and sin, stands in direct contradiction with the
cross of Christ, with faith in that Jesus who for
this cause was crucified that he might free humanity from sin, so that all who attach themselves to
him should now be crucified to sin, to the world,
to themselves. The whole carnal, sinful life of
such persons, who, as far as in them lay, made void
the very object for which Jesus was crucified,
might be called enmity to the cross of Christ. We
grant that what follows might also be understood,
as directed against men of this carnal course of
life. Still we are led by the connection, when
compared with the preceding context, to refer it
rather to an opposition manifesting itself in the
doctrines taught as well as in the life, to that very
class of Judaizing adversaries indeed, against
whom Paul has previously spoken. These he calls
enemies of the cross of Christ, because their stand-
point is one to which Christ the Crucified is an offence, a stone of stumbling—though in them this
manifests itself not openly and consciously, but

rather in an unconscious and covert manner; because nothing was more offensive to them than
that preaching which required them to ascribe
salvation to the Crucified Jesus alone as their Saviour,—to ascribe all to Him alone ; because they
held to a legal self-righteousness in opposition to
the cross of Christ. It follows from what has already been said, that the views and conduct of
such persons were in direct contrast to the worship of God in the spirit; their religious service
consisting only in external things, their tendency
being wholly to the earthly and sensual. Such a
religion brought with it no moral transformation,
might co-exist with sin, nay, might form a union
with it, giving to the service of sin a false security; as often, in the history of Christianity, we
have seen these same tendencies gain a footing
under cover of its name. He describes them as
those whose god is their belly, those who in all
things act merely from earthly impulses, to satisfy
their sensual wants; a reproach which Paul often
casts upon the judaizing proselytists, that they
turned their preaching into a means of gain, seeking to extort by it what might serve for their own
advantage. He describes them as earthly-minded,

which is explained by the foregoing; and all their
hopes were such as corresponded to this earthly
disposition. They expected in the future world,
as they did in the thousand years' reign promised
by them, not that divine life of which the true
Christian even here partakes under the veil of the
earthly; but, on the contrary, they dreamed of an
increased enjoyment of mere earthly pleasures.
"Whose glory," he says, "is in their shame," i. e.
who seek their honor in that which redounds
rather to their shame; as indeed everything,
which might seem to distinguish them above
others, was in fact a derogation of the Christian
life, a renunciation of true Christian excellence.

In contrast with these, Paul now presents the
wholly heavenward mind of the genuine Christian, his wholly heavenward hope purified from
every stain of sense. This divine life, already
freed from earth, forms in its aim and tendency
the opposite of that world-ensnared religiosity,
cleaving wholly to the earthly. This earthly
mind, Paul would say, must be far from us who
are Christians; "for our conversation is in
Heaven." His meaning is, that Christians, as to
their life, their walk, belong even now to Heaven;

in the whole direction of their life existing there
already. This he deduces from their relation to
Christ, their fellowship with him to whom they are
inseparably united, so that where he is there are
they also. While here, they are sustained by the
consciousness that Christ now lives in Heaven,
manifested to believers, though hidden from the
world. Thither is their gaze directed, as their long-
ings rise towards a Saviour, who will come again
from thence to make them wholly like himself, to
fashion them wholly after his own glorious pattern, to transform them wholly into the heavenly.
Hence Paul says: "From whence also we look for
the Saviour, the Lord Jesus Christ; who shall
change our vile body, that it may be fashioned like
unto his glorious body, according to the working
whereby he is able even to subdue all things unto
himself." There is not presented here a resurrection, as a restoration merely of the same earthly
body in the same earthly form; but, on the contrary,
a glorious transformation, proceeding from the
divine, the all-subduing power of Christ; so that
believers, free from all the defects of the earthly existence, released from all its barriers, may reflect the
full image of the heavenly Christ in their whole glo-

rified personality, in the soul pervaded by the divine life and its now perfectly assimilated glorified organ. This heavenly form of the Christian hope, the fruit of faith in the risen and ascended Jesus, stands opposed not only to that comfortless unbelief, which makes man a perishable creature like to the brutes, and cuts off all hope of what is beyond the earth; but also, as intended in this passage, to that mere carnal hope which transfers the forms of earthly existence into the future life. Both are scions from one root, the tendency of the natural man; who, whether in the form of sensual grossness or of refined culture, can never escape beyond the narrow limits of time and sense; who has no organ whereby to perceive and comprehend the divine and heavenly. It matters not, therefore, in which of these two forms this tendency of the natural man develops itself; whether it entirely denies and rejects what it cannot perceive and comprehend, denies all personal duration beyond the earthly state, because able itself to conceive nothing beyond this earthly form of personality; or whether it degrades to its own sensual standard what it is either unable or indisposed to deny, and wholly carnalizes the hope which

it does not reject. In every form of superstition
there is something of unbelief, since that upward
impulse of the spirit is wanting by which alone it
is possible to rise to the superhuman and divine;
hence the divine, as such, is in reality denied and
the earthly set in its place. And in all the forms
of unbelief there is something of superstition.
Every form of unbelief has its idols. It seeks in
the powers and outward phenomena of the world,
what can only be found in God and in powers
which are of God. What Paul says of the idol-
izing of worldly objects is true also of this, that
it makes itself subject to the elements of the
world. It clings with all the greater force to the
earthly, because it is an utter stranger to all which
can give true satisfaction to the spirit formed in
the image of God. It strives all the more eagerly
for earthly interests, because it has renounced the
higher interests pertaining to the spirit, which are
connected with its true home; and hence the
earthly interest has swallowed up all other love,
and all other desire, by which the God-related
spirit is impelled. Christ, risen from the dead and
ascended to heaven, whose life is hid in God and
with whom in God our life is hidden (Col. iii. 3),

to whom as our life we shall be like in glory when
He, now hidden from the world, shall reveal himself in glory,—this, the believer's hope, stands in
contrast with both these tendencies of the natural man.

We have spoken of the judaistic tendency existing at this stage of the development of Christianity, so far as this stood directly opposed to the
pure Gospel and excluded all reconciliation.   But
there were also in the churches, such as were in a
process of progressive development from Judaism,
or some kindred stand-point, to the pure Gospel.
These, far from being enemies of the cross of
Christ, were filled with love to the Crucified Jesus
as their Saviour; but they were still subject to
many weaknesses in their faith, not being able to
release themselves as yet from much which still
clung to them of their former, not wholly extir-
pated Jewish views.   Such persons, whom Paul is
accustomed to contrast as "the weak" with the
strong mature Christian, are often mentioned in
his Epistles; those who still had scrupulous fears
about partaking of meats offered to idols, and who,
in regard to food and to the observance of certain
days as holy, were still in bondage to the Jewish

ritual. In these points they were unable to break loose at once from the yoke of Judaism. But did these persons then stand in the same relation as those first-mentioned? Should such as had come over to Christianity from another stand-point, the pagan; and who, though exposed to other dangers, could from that point make their way more easily to Christian freedom; or such as had advanced farther in the development of faith, had more nearly reached the maturity of manhood in Christ; should such withdraw fellowship from, and harshly repel these weaker, in many points less enlightened brethren? This would have been contrary to what Paul requires of Christian love, which bears patiently the infirmities of brethren. It would be to set bounds with impatient presumption to the operations of the Holy Spirit, who is able to lead on farther and farther those in whom He has begun to work; to sever at once the thread of development ordained by the wisdom of God, and alone conducting to Christ as from him it proceeded. How we are to regard and treat these subordinate stages of development, these minor differences, is taught by Paul in this epistle,—in few words indeed, but full of

instruction.   We must now endeavor to obtain **a**
clear conception of their import.

After having, in a passage already explained,
presented as the standard for all, that stage of
Christian attainment which forgets everything
hitherto accomplished; which, beginning with
Christian faith, in entire devotedness to Christ
strives ever towards the mark of the heavenly
calling; he adds, " As many of us now as are perfect, let us be thus minded."   This is the stage of
the mature believer who has attained to full Christian freedom, who presses forward without hin-
drance in an ever-progressive development. "And
if in anything ye are otherwise minded,"—otherwise, i. e. not in harmony with this principle,—
" God will reveal also this unto you;" will also in
that, wherein ye still think otherwise, reveal to
you the right, and thus lead you to unity in adherence to this principle and in its application.
Paul refers therefore to the great truth, that the
Spirit of God which has revealed to them the light
of the Gospel, will also carry on and complete this
his revelation in them, even to that point of Christian maturity; that He will continually advance
them in Christian knowledge; and where they are

still in error and divided in opinion, there too will
He yet make known to them the one true way.
They should therefore not contend with overhasty
zeal; as by this course one is easily estranged
more and more widely from another, easily hardened in opposing views through obstinate adherence to what has been once adopted. Still less
should they mutually condemn one another, but
rather seek to preserve that unity of the Christian
spirit which is above all these minor differences;
while all submitting to the common guide, the
Holy Spirit, should entrust themselves and one
another mutually to Him, the best Teacher, to be
led on continually under his guidance. As this
work has in all the same divinely laid foundation,
so should the farther development and the progressive purification of the divine work in each,
be left to the operation of the Holy Spirit by
whom it is first begun in each. There should be
no attempt to do violence, by any external influence, to the peculiar development of another,
which must follow its own laws grounded in his
peculiar personality; or to substitute something
forced on him from without, for the free development proceeding from within. This would be

6*

nothing else than attempting, by human arts of persuasion, (which yet have no power to penetrate to the inmost spirit, unless they find a point of connection in the existing attainments of the individual man) to accomplish that which can be wrought only by the Holy Spirit, that inward Teacher, whom all follow without constraint and in perfect harmony with their own freedom. It is only the action of the same leaven of divine truth, that can produce the same results in all; of that leaven which by degrees shall penetrate the whole spiritual life, purifying it from every foreign element. And if there is reference here to a REVELATION by the Holy Spirit, through which the believer is advanced in knowledge, it is based on the truth everywhere expressed or pre-supposed in the Holy Scriptures, that all divine things can become known only in the light of the Holy Spirit: as Paul elsewhere says, "No man can say that Jesus is the Lord, but by the Holy Ghost." But the idea of revelation in this passage nowise excludes the activity of human thought, which still farther develops and works out, according to the laws of human reason, what has been received by divine illumination. This activity of the human

spirit is, however, pre-supposed to be one animated
and guided by the Holy Spirit, who is the vital
principle in the whole spiritual life; and hence all
is here referred back to the Holy Spirit as the
primary source, inasmuch as all is here the fruit of
its illuminating, guiding and quickening influence;
and all progressive Christian insight, whether immediately or mediately proceeding from the Holy
Spirit, is comprehended in the idea of revelation.

We must now more particularly consider tha.
which Paul makes the necessary condition of this
result, viz. that all should yield themselves to the
guidance of the Holy Spirit, and thus be led on
by him in progressive Christian knowledge. Buf
here it is necessary to inquire into the origina.
form of Paul's words. The passage has been cor
rupted, by introducing into the text marginal ex
planations erroneously supposed to be the word
of Paul. Divine Wisdom has not seen fit to guar
against such corruptions in the course of ages, bj
a series of miracles, or by the authority of ;
visible church enjoying infallible guidance. Bu
while free course was here given to natural cause
and thus such corruptions might occur throug]
misapprehension, this was to become the stimu

lus to an independent spirit of inquiry, and to
the cultivation also of all those mental faculties
whereby we test and discriminate. By such exercise, under the guidance of the Holy Spirit, by
the culture and application of that capacity to
which we give the name of CRITICISM, and which is
one of the natural endowments of the human
mind, we were to learn to distinguish the true
from the false, and by comparison to ascertain the
original form of the Apostolic words. Even criticism, under the guiding and quickening influence
of the Holy Spirit, belongs to the spiritual gifts
of the church. By it we shall be able here to
restore the true form of Paul's words; as by continued investigations, under the guidance of the
Holy Spirit, a harmony of views in this respect
may at length be attained throughout the church.

If like Luther we follow the later reading, we
shall translate with him,—"At least so far as we
walk after one rule whereto we have attained, and
are like-minded." According to this, unity is here
pointed out as that condition of which we have
just spoken; it is an exhortation to unity. Such
a thought, however, is quite remote from this
connection. Unity is not the condition which the

connection would lead us to expect; but, on the contrary, is that which results from the course of conduct required of the church by Paul. When all conduct, in reference to minor differences, as Paul according to our explanation has directed, unity will be maintained unimpaired in the church Moreover, what is said of "the one rule" and of "the walking together in accordance therewith," of "being like-minded," does not suit well with the words "whereto we have attained." All had not as yet attained to the same grade of spiritual discernment. We find here, therefore, a combination of words unsuited to each other; and it is easy to perceive, how from false glosses appended in explanation of the obscure words (obscure when not rightly apprehended in their connection) "if we do but walk after that whereto we have attained" falsely regarded as an exhortation to unity, all the rest may have originated. We shall, therefore, following the oldest manuscripts that have come down to us, regard these as the genuine words of Paul: "if we but walk according to that whereunto we have attained;" i. e. if each one but faithfully applies to his own life the measure of spiritual discernment bestowed upon him. This then is Paul's meaning: the Holy Spirit will reveal to all whatever is still wanting to them in true Christian knowledge, and thus continually promote the union of their spirits, by purging away whatever foreign elements may still impair it; will from still existing differences develop a higher unity, if first of all that Christian fellowship, which rests upon the one common ground of faith, is firmly adhered to, and each one is careful to put in practice with strict fidelity his own measure of Christian knowledge, without contending with others about matters wherein they differ from himself. All progressive revelation of the Spirit, all new light of which man is made partaker, presupposes a faithful application of what has previously been given. Here too apply the words of the Lord, " He that hath, to him shall be given." How many schisms might have been avoided in the church, how many differences might, much for its interest, have been overcome and adjusted, if all had felt the obligation rightly to understand and apply the principle here laid down by Paul !

In Paul's Epistles, as everywhere in the Holy Scriptures, precepts, exhortations, and promises go hand in hand. This must be so, from the peculiar

nature of the Gospel as distinguished from the
Law. For as all promises are connected with
some condition without which they cannot be fulfilled, and this leads to precepts and admonitions;
so would these be of no avail were not the
promise to the believer presupposed, that promise which ensures the power to fulfil what is
required of him. Thus Paul begins with the
words, "Rejoice in the Lord always; and again I
say rejoice." He, the prisoner of the Lord, looking it may be to a near approaching death, finds
reason to promise and to require an ever-abiding
joy in the consciousness of fellowship with the
Lord; to make joy indeed the ground-tone of the
Christian life, to make the whole Christian life a
jubilee of redemption. But with this connects
itself the requisition for a Christian walk; since
that joy in the Lord cannot exist, if the life of
the Christian does not correspond to the law of
the Lord, does not testify of fellowship with him.
And since the Philippians, as we have already
seen,* were placed in circumstances in which they
might most easily be tempted to anger and retali-
ation, if the natural man were not held in check

* See p. 24.

by a higher power, Paul especially urges the admonition, "Let your moderation be known unto all men;" and adds, "The Lord is at hand," appealing to the consciousness that He is ever near.[*] This consciousness furnishes the motive to such gentleness under provocation. They walk in the sight of the Lord, and dare not give way to passion in the near presence of Him, who endured every wrong with heavenly patience and long-suffering. This consciousness that the Lord is near, will also restrain them from wishing to anticipate his justice, to take the work of retribution into their own hands.—But these words also form the transition to what follows,—to the requirement "Be careful for nothing." Here too we must take into account the miserable state of the oppressed Christians; and yet they were to be careful for nothing, in the consciousness that the Lord is near. Not all human care is forbidden by Paul, who himself, as we have already seen,[†] in this very Epistle lays claim to earnest human efforts. But

* This might indeed be understood as referring to time, viz. the nearness of his coming, towards which the Apostles and the apostolic age, overlooking all that intervened, directed their longing desire. But this idea, though appropriate in some points of view, is obviously less suited to the whole connection than the one which we have exhibited in the text.

† See p. 77.

such entanglement in cares as stands in contradiction with that requirement, "to rejoice always in
the Lord,"—this is forbidden by him, from this
should the conscious nearness of the Lord restrain
the believer. Instead of indulging such care, he
directs them rather to raise the soul to God, and
all shall become light. The true meaning of these
words appears from the contrast which follows:
'But, in all things, make your requests known to
God in prayer and supplication with thanksgiving." There is a carefulness which is inconsistent
with confiding prayer to God, which excludes the
spirit of filial supplication. Such a carefulness
Paul forbids. As he had made the whole Christian life a joy in the Lord, so now he makes it
also a perpetual prayer. The two stand in inti-
mate connection. Neither can exist without the
other. He does not require the suppression of
those wants, the sense of which begets anxiety,
but that the sense of want should take the form
of prayer. Thus will the burdened spirit become
lightened, and care of itself will fall away. Yet,
although the Christian has wants to spread out
before God in prayer, and much to ask of Him for
the future, he still finds in every situation enough

that calls for thankfulness to God, since all things work together for good to those who love Him. Paul had already enjoined on the Philippians, afflicted as they were, to rejoice always in the Lord; and in this it is assumed that there is nothing unreasonable in the requirement, that they should give thanks to God. The whole Christian life should be a prayer, the prayer of thanksgiving and of supplication, in the consciousness of grace received and the conscious need of renewed grace. Assuming that the Philippians followed these directions, he could impart to them the precious promise which assured their safety in all conflicts: "And the peace of God which passes all understanding, shall keep your hearts and minds through Christ Jesus."—What does Paul here say? What is the sense, so far as we can indicate it in brief, of his deep and sublime words? If the Philippians so conduct, then will that peace with God, which they have received from Christ, remain with them; that peace which is the fountain of all other peace; which can exist in the midst of conflict with the world, and can be disturbed by no other power; that peace of which Jesus spake (John xiv. 27), "Peace I leave with you,

my peace I give unto you; not as the world
giveth give I unto you." And hence he adds, for
those whom he left behind amidst the conflicts of
the world, the consoling promise, "Let not your
heart be troubled, nor let it be afraid." This
peace, as it has God for its author, Paul accordingly describes as a peace which is above all
human conception. He who has this peace has
more than he himself knows, more than he is able
to set forth in thoughts and words. It is an over-
flowing heavenly repose, with which nothing
earthly can be compared; which fills the spirit of
him, who, having been reclaimed from disunion
with the Infinite and the Holy One, is now conscious of being in harmony with Him. The power
of this peace, says Paul, will conduct the souls that
live in fellowship with Christ, safe and unharmed
through all conflicts and assaults from within and
from without. From this proceeds the ground-
tone of their thoughts and feelings, this is their
protection, which avails against all human care.
With this may be compared the words of Paul in
the Epistle to the Colossians:* "And the peace
of God rule in your hearts!" The peace with God

* Chap. iii. 15.

procured to the believer through Christ, the peace which has its life in God, of which they are assured in union with him,—that peace, amid all fluctuation, is the controlling, the determining element in the Christian life.

THE END.

R